THE JPS BIBLE COMMENTARY

JONAH יוֹנָה

The JPS Torah Commentary

GENERAL EDITOR   *Nahum M. Sarna*
LITERARY EDITOR   *Chaim Potok*

GENESIS   *Nahum M. Sarna*
EXODUS   *Nahum M. Sarna*
LEVITICUS   *Baruch A. Levine*
NUMBERS   *Jacob Milgrom*
DEUTERONOMY   *Jeffrey H. Tigay*

The JPS Bible Commentary

The Five Megillot and Jonah
GENERAL EDITOR   *Michael Fishbane*

JONAH   *Uriel Simon*

THE JPS BIBLE COMMENTARY

JONAH יוֹנָה

The Traditional Hebrew Text with the New JPS Translation
Commentary by U R I E L S I M O N

Translated from the Hebrew by Lenn J. Schramm
The new JPS translation adapted by Uriel Simon

 T H E   J E W I S H   P U B L I C A T I O N   S O C I E T Y

PHILADELPHIA   1 9 9 9 / 5 7 6 0

The Jewish Publication Society
2100 Arch Street, 2nd floor
Philadelphia, PA 19103-1399

Composition by El Ot Ltd. (English text) and Varda Graphics (Hebrew text)
Design by Adrianne Onderdonk Dudden
Manufactured in the United States of America

06 8 7 6 5 4

Library of Congress Cataloging-in Publication Data

Bible. O.T. Jonah. Hebrew. 1999.
    *Jonah : the traditional Hebrew text with the new JPS
translation / commentary by Uriel Simon ; translated from
the Hebrew by Lenn J. Schramm.*
        p. cm.—(JPS Bible commentary)
        Includes bibliographical references.
        ISBN 0-8276-0672-9
        *I. Bible O. T. Jonah—Commentaries. I. Simon, Uriel. II. Schramm, Lenn
J.   III. Bible. O. T. Jonah. English. Jewish Publication Society. 1999. IV. Title.
V. Series.*
BS1602.S56   1999   99-28376
223'.92077—dc21   CIP

GENESIS   ISBN 0-8276-0326-6
EXODUS   ISBN 0-8276-0327-4
LEVITICUS   ISBN 0-8276-0329-0
NUMBERS   ISBN 0-8276-0329-0
DEUTERONOMY   ISBN 0-8276-0330-4
Five-volume set   ISBN 0-8276-0331-2
JONAH   ISBN 0-8276-0672-9
ESTHER   ISBN 0-8276-0699-0

First Hebrew edition, Jerusalem and Tel Aviv, 1992
German translation of the first edition, Stuttgart, 1994
English translation of the revised and expanded Hebrew edition, Philadelphia, 1999

CONTENTS

PREFACE

Each generation produces its own Bible commentaries, in accordance with what it finds perplexing, its exegetical methods, and its emotional and spiritual needs. A generation that shirks its duty of reinterpretation is shutting its ears to the message that the Bible has to offer. The gates of exegesis are not shut and never will be; each generation has its own special key, which corresponds to one of the seventy facets of the Bible. The present commentary has been written under the sign of a dual commitment: academic rigor, which aims at uncovering the original meaning of the Book of Jonah; and a Jewish commitment to Scripture as the taproot of our national existence and wellspring of our religious life.

It is a great privilege to have been called upon to forge another link in the long chain of Jewish biblical exegesis, which goes back to the ancient versions and midrashim of the sages, passes through the classical exegetes of the Middle Ages, and continues in contemporary research in Israel and the Diaspora. May this commentary be a worthy link in this glorious chain, so that future generations relate to the Book of Jonah through it, just as I have done through the efforts of my predecessors.

The cumulative scholarship of the generations passes from commentator to commentator. The latest, who stands on the shoulders of his predecessors, chooses whatever suits the goal he has set himself and the method he has adopted. To cite each and every gloss in the name of its originator would have made the commentary exceedingly unwieldy. Accordingly I have given source references only for those opinions and insights that are clearly the innovations of specific scholars. With regard to the abundant material that has passed into the public domain, readers are referred to the bibliography, which includes all the commentaries and studies on which the present commentary is based.

The commentary divides the Book of Jonah into seven literary units. Each is prefaced by the "Traditional Hebrew Text with the New JPS Translation" (1985). In order to eliminate any tension between that translation and the commentary, however, the JPS rendering has been modified to match the commentary in those places where the translators understood the Hebrew text differently than I do, where I felt a need to bring out certain idiomatic qualities of the Hebrew original, and where the translators' elegant variation conceals the repetition of key words in the Hebrew original. I acknowledge that these modifications come at the expense of the elegance and contemporary sound of the translation.

The commentary printed here is in fact a second, revised and expanded edition of the Hebrew original, which appeared as part of the series *Mikra Leyisra'el: A Bible Commentary for Israel* (Jerusalem and Tel Aviv, 1992). Readers should be aware of the great contribution made by editors of that series, Moshe Greenberg and Shmuel Ahituv, to the present commentary. They sketched out the format, laid down firm principles, paid close attention to details great and small, noted omissions and superfluities, and demanded maximum accuracy from the work while recognizing the ultimate responsibility of the author.

I would also like to thank my translator, Lenn Schramm, for his faithful and accurate English rendering, as well as for some useful points he raised in the margins of his draft.

I dedicate this volume to my wife Shulamit, who helped me adhere to the true purpose of the commentary and not yield to the temptation to run away to Tarshish.

Uriel Simon
Jerusalem, Sivan 5759 / June 1999

INTRODUCTION

The Theme of the Book and the History of Its Exegesis

Biblical narrative tends to prefer indirect expression over explicit ideological, ethical, or psychological statements. This tendency reaches its most radical manifestation in the Book of Jonah. As a result, it is particularly difficult to identify the central theme that unites all the elements of the story into a literary and conceptual whole. The broad variety of opinions on this subject—from the talmudic sages through modern commentaries—can be subsumed under four basic headings. Each offers its own answer to the three interrelated questions: Why was Jonah unwilling to prophesy against Nineveh? What did the Lord teach His prophet by means of the tempest, the fish, and the gourd? What are readers supposed to learn from the book?

Atonement versus Repentance   The designation of Jonah as the *haftarah* for the Afternoon Service of the Day of Atonement (B. Megillah 31a) reflects the view that this book depicts the concept of repentance so starkly and completely that it can stir hearers to repent of their ways and even modify their conduct. The Ninevites' repentance does indeed seem to be an exemplary combination of fasting, prayer, and deeds (abandoning their evil ways), just as its acceptance by the merciful God is tantamount to a guarantee and confirmation that authentic repentance has the power to nullify the fatal decree. Accordingly, the return of the people of Nineveh from their evil ways is cited as an example to be included in the admonition delivered by the elder on the occasion of a public fast (M. Ta'anit 2,1). The sages go further and magnify its extent beyond the bare statement of the text: "What is meant by 'and from the injustice which is in his hands' (3:8)? Samuel said: 'Even someone who had stolen a beam and built it into his house destroyed the entire building and returned the beam to its owner'" (B. Ta'anit 16a; compare *Midrash Jonah,* ed. Jellinek, pp. 100–102; ed. Horovitz, pp. 19–20; and see Maimonides' Code, the *Mishneh Torah,* Laws of Theft and Loss 1,5). According to Yehezkel Kaufmann, "Jonah is the classic statement of the Israelite idea of repentance" (p. 285), which aims to reject the ancient view, expressed by Jonah's unwillingness to warn the transgressors and his protest against the clemency shown them, that only punishment can cleanse sin. Like the Book of Job, this is a book of rebellion and protest, "except that Jonah complains that divine mercy detracts from divine justice, whereas Job complains that divine anger infringes upon divine justice" (p. 284).

Were repentance the thread that unites the book, we could expect that all its episodes would relate to it, in some fashion or other. Yet only chapter 3 deals with this theme. Unlike the people of Nineveh, the sailors are not described as transgressors;

consequently their submission to the will of the Lord and their great reverence for Him do not constitute a turning back from sin. Jonah does indeed sin, but his prayer from the belly of the fish is quite devoid of contrition, while his silence at the end of the book leaves the extent of his change outside the narrative. Most importantly, the attempts by Kaufmann (ibid.) and Bickerman (p. 41) to interpret the prophet's protest against the divine attributes of compassion, mercy, and repenting of evil (4:2) as a moral protest against the atoning power of repentance are too limited to encompass the full complexity of the theme. Evidence of this is that the incident of the plant and the Lord's reply to Jonah (4:6–11) clearly relate to quite a different subject: Nineveh merits its Creator's protection not because of its citizens' remorse, but because it is a great metropolis, teeming with children who have never sinned, and many beasts as well.

Universalism versus Particularism   The second view is that Jonah preferred loyalty to his people Israel over his duty to obey the Lord of the universe, his master. For this approach, the key to the story is that it is set exclusively among gentiles, who are presented in a positive light. Not only is Jonah dispatched to bring the word of the Lord to a gentile metropolis, whose citizens are astonishingly quick to repent; even the crew of the ship, who represent many nations and languages, astonish us with their religious and moral sensitivity. Against this background, the Hebrew prophet's refusal to go to Nineveh is explained by his fear that the anticipated repentance of the gentile city will cast a heavy shadow on the stiff-necked Israelites. According to this interpretation, the Book of Jonah is meant to extirpate the particularistic belief that regards the welfare of Israel as a supreme value and to assert that the prophet's love for his people must not keep him from fulfilling the mission imposed by the one universal God, as Elisha did when he was sent to Hazael, the enemy of Israel (2 Kings 8:9–15).

This view can be traced back to a midrash:

> Jonah said, "I will go outside the Land of Israel, to a place where the Divine Presence is not revealed, so as not to render Israel guilty"—because the Gentiles are quick to repent. . . .
>
> There were thus three prophets: one asserted the dignity of the father [i.e., God] and the dignity of the son [i.e., Israel]; one asserted the dignity of the father but not the dignity of the son; and one asserted the dignity of the son but not the dignity of the father. Jeremiah asserted the dignity of the father and the dignity of the son. . . . For this reason his prophecy was repeated. . . . Elijah asserted the dignity of the father and not the dignity of the son. . . . And what is said there? "The LORD said to him, '. . . anoint Elisha son of Shaphat of Abel-meholah to succeed you as prophet'" (1 Kings 19:15–16)—"to succeed you" means "I do not want your prophecy." Jonah asserted the dignity of the son and not the dignity of the father, as it says, "Jonah arose to flee" (1:3), followed by "the word of the LORD came to Jonah a second time" (3:1)—He spoke with him a second time, but not a third time! Rabbi Nathan says: Jonah went only to throw himself into the sea, as it is stated, "Lift me and cast me into the sea" (1:12). So too you find that the Patriarchs and the prophets gave themselves on behalf of Israel. . . . (*Mekhilta of Rabbi Ishmael*, Masekhta de-Pisḥa, §1, ed. Horovitz-Rabin, pp. 3–4)

This interpretation was adopted by Rashi, Joseph Kara, David Kimḥi (who combined it with the third theme presented below), and Abraham ibn Ezra. Don Isaac Abravanel, however, demurs: "It is in truth a very weak interpretation, since the repentance of the people of Nineveh might make Israel ashamed of their sins, so that they would return to the Lord who would have mercy on them" (preface to his commentary on Jonah, Second Question). Abravanel offers, instead, the same idea, but in its political version: Jonah—whom he assumes to have survived until after the campaigns (734–732 B.C.E.) by the Assyrian king Tiglath-Pileser III in the Transjordan and the Galilee (see his commentary on 1:1 and 3:4)—refused to save Nineveh "because he knew the evils and exiles that it would bring on the tribes of Israel in the future; hence he yearned that the nation of Assyria be destroyed and Nineveh its capital be utterly smitten. This is why he fled instead of going there" (Introduction, "The Overall Intention").

This view has no substantial anchor in the text. Its keystone—the prophet's willingness to give his life rather than expose his people's stubbornness to God and man, or in order to prevent the salvation of the power destined to destroy Israel—is simply not to be found in the book. Hardly any Jewish Bible scholar still adheres to this exegetical line, but it remains attractive to most Christian scholars. Urbach (pp. 119–121) noted the striking similarity between the midrash that juxtaposes the Ninevites' immediate response to a single prophet with the indifference of the people of Jerusalem to many prophets (Lamentations Rabbah, Introduction, 31), on the one hand, and Jesus' remark that the people of Nineveh who responded to Jonah's call were superior to the people of his own generation, who ignored him (Matt. 12:41; Luke 11:32). Urbach concludes from this similarity that the self-criticism in the Jewish homily was appropriated by Christian thought and intensified in the anti-Jewish strictures of the Church fathers St. Jerome (c. 342–c. 420) and Ephrem Syrus (306–373) (whose homily on the repentance of the people of Nineveh has them say, "Praise be to God, who mortified the Jews by means of the gentiles"). In the modern scholarly version of this christological exegesis, the Book of Jonah is described as a polemic against the narrow exclusivism prevalent among the returnees to Zion that resulted from the travails of the destruction of the First Temple, the exile, and Persian domination. According to this position, the election of Israel requires the Jews to turn away from members of other nations and even justifies disdain for them. Jonah is accordingly taken as the representative of this antipathy toward gentiles, and his flight is explained as a refusal to show them the way to repentance and salvation. The forceful blocking of his flight, by contrast, is meant to point us toward the true meaning of election: Israel was chosen to serve as the carrier of faith in order to disseminate it among all nations. To demonstrate that this awesome mission can be realized, the humble spirit and open heart of the gentiles aboard the ship and in Nineveh are juxtaposed with the arrogance of the prophet who rejects his mission.

This universalist view, too, cannot be anchored in the text of Jonah, unless one can show that the prophet is characterized as the embodiment of such Israelite exclusivism, whereas the sailors and people of Nineveh are cast as faithful representatives of the pagan gentile world and its openness to the call of faith. Although there seems to be some basis for this in Jonah's self-identification as a Hebrew who fears the Lord (1:9), his statement fits perfectly into the plot as a natural response to his interrogation by the sailors, who are trying to avoid shipwreck by unmasking the guilty party and the deity who is hounding him. Jonah's anger at the pardon extended to Nineveh might be taken as an indication that he is a xenophobe who longs for the destruction of idolaters. But this explanation is refuted by his conduct during the storm: instead of trying to force his pursuer to drown all those aboard the ship on account of his own transgression, he acts to prevent their being dragged into his quarrel with his God. In view of the absence of any manifestation of hatred for gentiles and idolatry (the book contains no condemnation of the sin of idolatry), it is impossible to interpret his self-stated reasons for running away (4:2) as a protest against the display of divine mercy toward idolaters. As Goitein insists (p. 97), had Jonah intended to protest the *scope* of God's mercy he would not have mentioned the attributes of compassion and kindness but used a phrasing similar to that of Ps. 145:9: "The LORD is good to all, and His mercy is upon all His works." Similarly, the Lord's response, through the incident of the plant and the explanation that follows it, is clearly intended to justify God's mercy in and of itself, since Jonah's painful recognition of his own dependence on the puny plant is irrelevant for someone who would deny gentiles any right to divine compassion. It is significant only for someone who holds that the Lord is to be censured, not praised, for His manifestations of mercy and compassion.

Thus Jonah does not symbolize Israel, and Nineveh does not symbolize the gentile world. What is more, the people of Israel and the kingdom of Assyria are not even mentioned in the book. Nineveh is described as a wicked city like Sodom, whose inhabitants deal unjustly with one another, and not as the capital of an empire enriched by plunder. The narrator makes no mention of its citizens' worship of idols, neither in the description of their sin nor in the account of their repentance. Hence it is impossible to explain Jonah's refusal to go to Nineveh as motivated by fear for the religious and spiritual or political and military well-being of Israel or by his opposition to the inclusion of gentiles in the kingdom of the Lord. It follows that the conspicuously gentile backdrop of the Book of Jonah has no panhumanist connotations and must be understood on the literary rather than the ideological level (see "The Literary Function of the Gentiles as Supporting Characters," p. xxxiv).

Prophecy: Realization versus Compliance   The third reading, which focuses on Jonah's stubborn refusal to prophesy against Nineveh and his anger at its deliverance, grounds the story on Jonah's jealous concern for the veracity of prophecy and his apprehension lest his credibility be undermined. The midrash illuminates Jonah's expectations by recalling his success in Samaria and his forebodings by a hypothetical reconstruction of his failure in Jerusalem:

> Why did he run away? The first time, God sent him to restore the territory of Israel and His word was fulfilled, as it is stated: "He [Jeroboam II] restored the territory of Israel from Lebo-hamath [in accordance with the promise that the LORD . . . made through His

servant,... Jonah son of Amittai]" (2 Kings 14:25). The second time, He sent him to Jerusalem to destroy it. Because [its people] repented, the Holy One Blessed be He acted in accordance with His great mercy and repented of His fatal intention and did not destroy it. Thus Israel called him a "false prophet." The third time, He sent him to Nineveh. Jonah reasoned with himself, saying, "I know that this nation is quick to repent. Now they will repent, and the Holy One Blessed be He will dispatch his anger against Israel. Is it not enough that Israel calls me a false prophet, but idol-worshippers will do so as well! I shall run away instead. . . ." (*Pirkei de-Rabbi Eliezer* 10)

According to this view—which was adopted by Daniel al-Kumissi the Karaite, Saadiah Gaon (*Beliefs and Opinions* 3,5), Rashi, Joseph Kara, and David Kimḥi (who combined it with the second theme reviewed above), Abraham bar Ḥiyya, Abravanel, and many modern scholars—the Book of Jonah seeks to teach us about the educational purpose of prophecies of doom (cf. Ezek. 3:16–21 and 33:1–9) through the medium of a story that criticizes a prophet who viewed announcing future events as his role and full realization of the prophecy as his only test. Jonah runs away because he cannot resolve two contradictions: between the categorization of prophecies that do not come to pass as "false prophecies" (Deut. 18:21–22) and the revocation of the verdict against Nineveh, in response to its repentance; and between the concept of God as unchanging and resolute (cf. Num. 23:19) and His attributes of compassion and forgiveness. Nevertheless the Lord compelled him to prophesy against Nineveh to teach him the paradoxical nature of true prophets, who "foretell punishment to make it unnecessary" (St. Jerome in his commentary on Ezek. 33:1, cited by Bickerman, p. 40).

Such a definition of the prophet's role is undoubtedly an appropriate and weighty theme for a prophetic narrative, but there is no real sign in the Book of Jonah of the prophet's anguish that his prediction did not come to pass, nor anything like this elsewhere in the Bible. This is why the author of the midrash quoted above had to assume that Jonah had previously been mocked by the people of Jerusalem, while Bickerman (p. 38) is forced to rely on a strained comparison with Jeremiah's distress (20:7–8) when he is ridiculed by the sinful inhabitants of Jerusalem, who, seeing that the word of the Lord is slow to be realized, persist in their transgressions. Hence it is not surprising that most commentators who consider contingent prophecy to be the theme of the book combine it with some other theme.

In addition to the absence of an adequate basis in the text, this prophetic theme is also beset by its literary implausibility, as Ibn Ezra points out: "Furthermore, how could the prophet disobey the word of the Lord out of fear that the people of Nineveh might call him a false prophet? How would this harm him, since he does not live among them? In addition, the people of Nineveh were not fools: why should the Lord send His prophet to them unless it was to get them to return to Him? But if they did not return, then the sentence against them would be executed. And if they knew that if they returned to the Lord He would repent of the evil, why should they call him a false prophet?" (commentary on 1:2). It is extremely unlikely that what is obvious to the people of Nineveh and their king (as well as to King Hezekiah vis-à-vis Micah the Morashtite and to the elders of Judah vis-à-vis Jeremiah [Jer. 26:17–19]) is a problem of life and death for the Hebrew prophet. What is more, relating the lesson of the plant to the question of Jonah's status as a prophet renders his character shallow and absurd, turning him into a stubborn, petty, and heartless man who would rather witness the destruction of a great city than have his prestige impaired. Such an imbalance between the seriousness of the theme and the shallowness of the protagonist would detract from the expressive power of the story and weaken the force of its message (unless we are dealing with a satire; see "Ironic Satire or Compassionate Irony?" p. xxiii).

Compassion: Justice versus Mercy   The fourth view is that Jonah argues on behalf of strict justice against the merciful God, who repents of His sentence. Punishment of sinners in accordance with their wickedness is demanded by strict justice and essential to deter transgressors, but allowing the judge to stand above the law undermines the authority of the law and dims the clarity of the doctrine of reward and punishment. To the advocate of strict justice it is clear that wickedness abounds not only because of the viciousness of evildoers, but also because the Judge of all the earth does not treat them with the full severity of the law. He must learn that the world can exist only through the unfathomable amalgam of justice and mercy, that fear of sin is produced not only by fear of punishment, but also by awe at the sublimity of salvation ("The men feared the LORD greatly" [1:16]; cf. 1 Kings 17:24) and by fascination with grace and absolution ("Yours is the power to forgive so that You may be held in awe" [Ps. 130:4]). If Jonah is to be rid of the notion that divine compassion expresses weakness of mind and softness of heart, he must experience the Lord's heavy hand directed against himself. He must realize that the God who shows clemency to malefactors makes no concessions to His prophet—who pretends to know better than his God how the world should be conducted. Jonah's willingness to die for his principles steeled his heart and nurtured his rebellion. Eventually he will understand that his death wish led the self-righteous prophet astray no less than lust for life perverted the pleasure-seeking people of Nineveh. Jonah foresaw both the submission of the evildoers of Nineveh, terrified by their impending destruction, and the acceptance of their repentance by the merciful God; but he was totally wrong to believe that he would be allowed to escape to Tarshish. Subsequent surprises undermine his pretense to knowledge—the fish that saves him from death but imprisons him in its belly until he gives up his flight and begins to pray; and the plant that saves him from his distress but vanishes as suddenly as it appeared, so that he can feel the pain of loss and open his heart to understand the Creator's love for His creatures. Only when the proponent of strict justice realizes his own humanity can he understand the fundamental dependence of mortals on human and divine mercy. The midrashic sages had Jonah express this recognition, in body language and words, in the answer they report he gave to the Lord's rhetorical question that concludes the book:

> Then he fell on his face and said: "Conduct Your world according to the attribute of mercy, as it is written: 'To the LORD our God belong mercy and forgiveness' (Dan. 9:9)" (*Midrash Jonah,* ed. Jellinek, p. 102; ed. Horovitz, p. 21).

The halakhic sages, by contrast, expressed the same exegetical view by appending to the Book of Jonah, when read as the *haftarah* of the Afternoon Service on the Day of Atonement, the last three verses of the Book of Micah (7:18–20), through which Jonah, as it were, recants his condemnation of the attributes of compassion and grace (Jon. 4:2) by reciting the praises of God, who desires to be gracious to His creatures and lighten the burden of their sins and transgressions:

> Who is a God like You, forgiving iniquity and remitting transgression; who has not maintained His wrath forever against the remnant of his own people, because He loves graciousness. He will take us back in love; He will cover up our iniquities. You will hurl all our sins into the depths of the sea. You will keep faith with Jacob, loyalty to Abraham, as You promised on oath to our fathers in days gone by.

Another midrash (though it has no direct connection with the Book of Jonah) gives the fullest expression of the contrast between divine justice, which is the attribute associated with the measured and rationed justice inscribed in the Torah, the prophetic books, Psalms, and Proverbs (personified as wisdom), on the one hand; and divine mercy, which reveals the goodness and righteousness of the living God, on the other:

> They asked the Torah: "How is the sinner to be punished?" It replied, "Let him bring a sacrifice and he will be pardoned."
> They asked prophecy: "How is the sinner to be punished?" It replied, "The person who sins, . . . he shall die" (Ezek. 18:4).
> They asked David: "How is the sinner to be punished?" He replied, "May sinners disappear from the earth and the wicked be no more" (Ps. 104:35).
> They asked Wisdom: "How is the sinner to be punished?" It replied, "Misfortune pursues sinners" (Prov. 13:21).
> They asked the Holy One Blessed be He: "How is the sinner to be punished?" He replied, "Let him do repentance, and I will accept it, as it is written: 'Good and upright is the LORD [; therefore He shows sinners the way]' (Ps. 25:8)" (J. Makkot 2,6, according to a genizah fragment published by Shlomo Wieder, *Tarbiz* 17 [1946], p. 133).

The reservations offered against the first three views do not apply to this last. The chief reason is that it is the only one that does not focus on a particular segment of the story; rather, it is compatible with the entire narrative from beginning to end and encompasses most of its elements. A comprehensive view of the story must integrate its theological and psychological aspects, since it is the way of narrative to express the intellectual theme in part through the character of the hero. The vast majority of commentators and students of the Book of Jonah still adhere to one of the first three readings or some combination thereof (see David Kimḥi on 1:1). Our interpretation, however, explains the plot, the characters, and the dialogue as embodying the primordial struggle between justice and mercy. The theoretical facets of this interpretation will be clarified in greater detail in the introductions to the last two sections of the book (4:1–5 and 4:6–11).

Jonah's Place in the Biblical Canon

The Book of Jonah is the fifth among the twelve Minor Prophets, preceded by Obadiah and followed by Micah and Nahum. The most ancient testimony to this placement is the scroll of the Minor Prophets found in Wadi Muraba'at, which dates from the beginning of the second century C.E. In the Septuagint, however, Micah is third, and Jonah is moved down to sixth, between Obadiah and Nahum. Both orders seem to have been determined by chronological considerations, but it is rather difficult to reconstruct them. There is no doubt that the Jonah of our book was identified with Jonah son of Amittai, who was active during the reign of Jeroboam son of Joash (Jeroboam II), king of Israel (2 Kings 14:25). Obadiah was placed before Jonah because it was attributed to Obadiah, Ahab's major-domo (1 Kings 18:3; see B. Sanhedrin 39a); or because, as suggested by M. Z. Segal (*Introduction to Scripture I* [third edition, Jerusalem 1952], pp. 12–13 [Hebrew]), his prophecy of the destruction of Edom referred to the defeat of Edom by King Amaziah of Judah (2 Kings 14:7; see *Seder Olam Rabbah* 20), who was contemporary with Jeroboam's father Joash. Micah, for his part, began his prophetic career during the reign of Jotham, Amaziah's grandson, and Nahum was dated to the reign of Manasseh, Jotham's great-grandson (*Seder Olam Rabbah* 20). In addition, Micah prophesied the fall of Assyria (5:4–5) and Nahum the destruction of Nineveh (2:4–3:19). Thus the placement of these two books after Jonah expresses the view that Assyria returned to its evil ways after its short-lived repentance in the time of Jonah.

A homily in Midrash Numbers Rabbah 18,17 (21) understands the phrase "captain of fifty" (Isa. 3:3) as referring to the captain of the fifty books of the Law, both oral and written, enumerated as follows: "The twenty-four books, plus eleven of the Minor Prophets—except for Jonah, which stands by itself [as one of the twenty-four]—and the six orders [of the Mishnah] and nine chapters of [the halakhic midrash] *Torat Kohanim,* for a total of fifty." The midrash requires the addition of eleven books to the twenty-four books of the biblical canon (a count that reckons the Minor Prophets as one book) and accordingly distinguishes the Book of Jonah from the others, evidently because it is so different from them. Jonah is indeed unique among the Later Prophets in that it is named for its protagonist (like the books of the Former Prophets and several books of the Hagiographa) rather than its author and that, rather than presenting prophecies or "pronouncements," it is the account of an incident in the life of a prophet. It seems, then, Jonah's adventure should have been incorporated into the Book of Kings, like the stories of Elijah and Elisha (before or after it reports the prophecy of Jonah son of Amittai to Jeroboam II). But the difference between Jonah, on the one hand, and Elijah and Elisha, on the other, is greater still, since Jonah's mission to the far-off gentile city—whose king is not named nor his era stated—is not interwoven into the history of Israel in any fashion whatsoever. The placement of the Book of Jonah in the biblical canon is thus striking evidence that, despite its narrative nature, it was not regarded as part of biblical historiography, but rather of the prophetic literature.

The Literary Genre

Story or History? In the accounts of prophetic deeds found in the Former Prophets, miracles are an integral part of the real world and occur on the same plane as other incidents. In this, the story of Jonah resembles them: just as the Lord commanded the ravens to feed Elijah (1 Kings 17:4), so He commands or "appoints") the great fish to swallow Jonah and the plant to save him in his predicament. The first attempt to integrate the miracles of Elijah and Jonah into the normal course of nature, by viewing the deviation as preordained in natural law, can be found in the midrash: "R. Jonathan said: 'The Holy One Blessed be He stipulated with the sea that it would split before Israel.'... R. Jeremiah son of Eleazar said: 'The Holy One Blessed be He made such a condition not only with the sea, but with everything that was created during the six days of creation.... I commanded the ravens to feed Elijah... and the fish to vomit forth Jonah'" (Genesis Rabbah 5,5; see also M. Avot 5,5). The doubts about the intrinsic possibility of such miracles emerged among the rationalist circles of the rabbis in Spain. Maimonides (*Guide of the Perplexed* 1,42) reports (without strong reservations) that "some of the Andalusians" preferred to understand that the widow's son revived by Elijah had not really died; Joseph ibn Caspi (on Jon. 1:1) cites (without stating his own opinion) the dispute about the factual veracity of the first two chapters of the Book of Jonah: "Know too that there are conjectures about all this story, that is, from here until 'it spewed Jonah out upon dry land' (2:11). Some say that it all took place while he was awake, while others say that it was all a dream and prophetic vision." The proponent of the second theory may have been Abraham ibn Ezra, who adopted the dream solution with regard to Hosea's marriage and seems to allude to it in his commentary on Jon. 1:1: "All the prophecies of all the prophets, except for Moses after the glory of the Lord passed before his face, were in visions and dreams." However, this is not a plausible resolution of the problem dealt with by Ibn Ezra (which was how a prophet can flee from God). Moreover, in his commentary on 2:1, Ibn Ezra reveals his opinion about the incident of the fish; namely, that the protracted stay inside the fish is the deviation from natural law, not the fact of Jonah's being swallowed: "It is not in human power to remain in the belly of a fish for an hour, and all the more so this number [three full days], except by a miracle" (see also his commentary on 4:6).

If Ibn Caspi was not referring to Ibn Ezra, perhaps he was thinking about Maimonides, who wrote that it is just as likely that a man who has not studied Torah will prophesy as that "an ass or frog might prophesy" (*Guide of the Perplexed* 2,32). Although Ibn Caspi, in his two commentaries on the *Guide of the Perplexed* (on the literal and esoteric meanings), does not interpret Maimonides's remark in this way, a century after him it was glossed precisely in this fashion by Profiat Duran: "This alludes to [Balaam's] ass and Jonah's fish, which cannot be understood literally, and were entirely in prophetic visions." This explanation was also adopted by his contemporary Shemtov ibn Shemtov. Don Isaac Abravanel, however, disagreed with both of them in his commentary on the *Guide* and offered compelling proofs that this was not Maimonides's intention. The allusion, then, seems to be spurious; nor can we reach a clear conclusion from what Maimonides wrote on the subject in two other passages: in one place he writes that the incident of Balaam's ass was "a prophetic vision" (2,42), while a few pages later (2,48) he relates to Jonah's fish as an actual event. In any case, whether Maimonides himself believed that the miracle of the fish was to be understood as a prophetic vision or literally, the Maimonidean school clearly tended to the former.

Exegetical rationalization makes the miracle unreal; scientific rationalization seeks to preserve it by demonstrating that it is compatible with natural law. In the latter spirit, there have been a number of attempts in the twentieth century to reconcile the miracle of Jonah's being swallowed by the fish and his protracted stay in its belly with human and cetacean anatomy and physiology. According to one approach, the large-toothed whales, especially sperm whales, have a wide and flexible pharynx that enables them to swallow even octopuses, and an air-breathing creature could survive in their stomach by virtue of their respiratory system. Others have suggested that human beings could survive even in species that have a narrow pharynx if conveyed into the large throat sac, where there is adequate room and air to breathe. Wilson endeavored to ground these anatomical speculations on the 1891 report of a sailor who was swallowed by a large sperm whale and survived in its stomach for a day and a night until his fellows cut open the dead whale and extracted him alive the next morning. Wilson (pp. 636–637) tried to force the facts and extend the sailor's stay inside the whale to almost three days and two nights, to bring it closer to Jonah's three days and three nights of captivity. But neither he nor those who follow in his wake seem to have known that the entire story had been refuted twenty years earlier and labeled a "sailor's tale" by the captain's wife (see *The Expository Times* 17 [1905/6], p. 521; 18 [1906/7], p. 239).

The repentance of the Ninevites, from a psychological standpoint, is less plausible than the physical possibility of the miracles that happened to Jonah. There is nothing like it anywhere else in the Bible. What is more, their repentance, unlike miracles, cannot be ascribed to divine intervention, because it is emphatically described as a human action (3:10). Isaiah went barefoot and naked for three years, trying to deter Judah from subscribing to the Assyrian alliance (Isaiah 20); but Jonah, who relied on no sign or portent, was heeded within a single day, even before two-thirds of the inhabitants of Nineveh could have heard his admonition directly from his mouth. The wondrous rapidity of their repentance is enhanced by its universal scope: "great and small alike" (3:5). Such unanimity in obedience to the word of God—achieved in Nineveh without any efforts at persuasion—is described by Jeremiah as a sign of the end of days, made possible then by an essential change in human nature: "I will put my teaching into their inmost being and inscribe it upon their hearts.... No longer will they need to teach one another and say to one another, 'Heed the LORD'; for all of them, from the least of them to the greatest, shall heed Me" (Jer. 31:33–34).

A number of midrashim question the sincerity of this repentance: "R. Shimon ben Lakish said: 'The repentance of the Ninevites was fraudulent'" (J. Taʿanit 2,1). R. Johanan expounded to their detriment the verse, "Let every person turn back from his evil ways and from the injustice which is in his hand" (3:8): "What was in their hands they returned, but not what was in the bureau, cupboard, or closet" (ibid.). This was not meant, though, as realistic exegesis that seeks to bring the repentance of Nineveh closer to reality, but as an apologetic attempt to erect a barrier against the Church fathers' tendentious use of the gentiles' repentance to assail the Jews (Urbach). On the other hand, a number of *peshat* (contextual-meaning) commentators did try to make the repentance of Nineveh more realistic, but they were forced to invoke extreme hypotheses. Abraham ibn Ezra (on 3:3) quotes from the lost commentary of the Jerusalem Karaite sage Yeshua ben Yehuda the clever suggestion (which, however, has no basis in the text) that prior general knowledge of the miracles at sea replaced a specific prophetic portent: "The crew of the ship went to Nineveh and reported their experience with Jonah, and this is why they believed him" (this idea may have been derived indirectly from Luke 11:30). Ibn Ezra's own hypothesis is more cautious; nor does he say whether it is offered as a supplement or substitute for the previous one: "It may be that [Jonah] was well known and his fame widespread, like Elisha [see 2 Kings 6:8–23; 8:7–15], and this is why they believed" (missing in the printed versions of the commentary but extant in manuscripts). Another and rather far-fetched conjecture of Ibn Ezra's, advanced in a different context (1:2), increases the reasonableness of Nineveh's repentance by greatly reducing the magnitude of its transgressions. The characterization of the city as "a great city to God" indicates that "they had feared the Lord formerly; but in Jonah's time they began to do evil. Had they not previously been of the Lord's party, why would He send His prophet to them? We see that they did perfect and unequaled repentance, yet you do not find that they shattered the altars of Baal or cut down idols. From this we can learn that they were not idol-worshippers." David Kimḥi (on 3:5) adopted Yeshua ben Yehuda's conjecture and ignored Ibn Ezra's two suggestions. All three commentators illustrate the difficulty of remaining faithful to the *peshat* if the repentance of Nineveh is taken as a historical event.

In addition to the question of the sincerity and theological plausibility of the repentance of Nineveh, we may ask about its historical likelihood: is it really conceivable that the prophet of the Lord, who comes from the small and distant kingdom of Israel, can influence the pagan metropolis to abandon its wicked and unjust ways? In the absence of any direct historical evidence of a change in Assyrian behavior in the first half of the eighth century B.C.E., scholars who answer this question in the affirmative (see the article by Wiseman) are forced to rely on indirect evidence to reconstruct a possible background for Jonah's mission to Nineveh: The kings and people of the neighboring kingdom of Mari are known to have heeded the advice and warnings of foreign experts in matters of medicine and religion; kings of Assyria took account of the prophecies of "seers" who accompanied foreign ambassadors to their court. Among the celestial portents that vexed the kings of Assyria to the point that they declared a public fast and temporarily renounced power in favor of a substitute were a total eclipse of the sun and a severe earthquake. Jonah, who was active during the reign of Jeroboam II (785–749 B.C.E.), might have exploited the full solar eclipse that occurred in the year 763 B.C.E., according to astronomical calculations, and in the tenth year of the reign of Esarhaddon III (671 B.C.E.), according to Assyrian annals. Alternatively, he could have exploited the severe earthquake that struck the region during the reigns of Jeroboam and Uzziah of Judah (Amos 1:1; Zech. 14:5). This earthquake should perhaps be identified with the tremor reported to have occurred during the reign of Esarhaddon (although the Assyrian text in question does not specify whether this was Esarhaddon III). This hypothetical historical reconstruction raises two literary questions: Why would the author of the Book of Jonah turn a quasi-diplomatic address to the royal court into a proclamation of the word of the Lord in the streets of the city? Why would he conceal the eclipse or earthquake that reinforced the prophet's warning and instead elevate the repentance of Nineveh into the far more sublime response to a simple call with no accompanying sign? Whatever gain these scholars make by buttressing the historical credibility of the event with extra-biblical evidence comes at the expense of undermining the value of the Book of Jonah as historiography. On the contrary, the fact that the realistic elements that historians find in external documents are patently absent from the story of Jonah strengthens the presumption of its non-historical nature.

The question of historical plausibility is really external to the story; how we answer it neither adds nor detracts from its literary and theological meaning. On the other hand, identifying the literary genre to which the book belongs is important for its exegesis. Is it a prophetic story like those of Elijah, clearly intending to narrate actual facts? Or is it a fictional tale like that of Job, intended to express theological verities in artistic language?

The Book of Jonah lacks the traditional hallmarks of historical writing. The name and country of the "king of Nineveh" are not indicated, nor is the deity he worshiped. As a result, the story is not anchored in a particular era and lacks a political dimension and cultic specification. The captain and his crew, each of whom calls upon his own god, also lack ethnic attribution and individuation. Jonah himself is identified with a known historical figure, but this identification seems to have been meant to characterize him and not to place him in the course of history (see "The Identification of Jonah with the Prophet Who Brought Good Tidings to Sinful Israel," p. xxxviii). This is true as well for the implied identification of the protagonist of the Book of Job with the well-known righteous man mentioned by Ezekiel (14:14 and 20). In a similar manner, Nineveh is not described as the capital of the Assyrian juggernaut but as a metropolis of injustice that lies somewhere in the east, just as the land of Uz, Job's home, is the country of the Kedemites, the illustrious sages and councilors (M. Weiss, *The Story of Job's Beginning* [Jerusalem 1983], pp. 21–24 [Hebrew]). The fact that the story ends with the Lord's rhetorical question, providing no information about the prophet's return home and the subsequent fate of Nineveh, strongly suggests that the story is no more biographical than it is historical. This utter lack of detail sets the story of Jonah poles apart from the Book of Esther, which is replete with names of persons and precise dates and concludes with information about the imposition of taxes throughout the Persian Empire and the lofty status of Mordecai in the government apparatus, both facts documented by reference to the chronicles of the kings of Persia and Media. In Esther, the theological aspect is hidden—divine providence works indirectly and under cover—so as to emphasize the historical and realistic aspect. In

Jonah, by contrast, the historical and realistic aspect is subdued in order to emphasize and intensify the theological point—that the Lord intervenes directly and overtly (Flusser).

One characteristic of nonrealistic writing is that the author is quite uninterested in whether the events described are possible and makes no attempt to buttress their plausibility. Thus the miracle of the fish focuses on the fact that Jonah is swallowed and spewed forth; the more difficult problem of his protracted stay in the belly of the fish, without air or food, is passed over in silence. Similarly, the miracle of the plant has to do with the shade that it provides to the prophet sitting east of Nineveh and its sudden decay; but we are left in the dark about where and how he may have obtained food and water (contrast the emphasis on the miraculous sources of food that sustain Elijah [1 Kings 17:2–16 and 19:4–8]). By the same token, the narrator does not think to tell us in what language the Hebrew prophet addresses the inhabitants of the distant city (unlike the stories of Joseph [Gen. 42:23] and of the Rabshakeh [2 Kings 18:26–28]). This means that the strikingly unrealistic nature of Jonah's rapid and sweeping influence over the large population of Nineveh—augmented by the fact that Jonah foresaw it with complete confidence (4:2)—is not an isolated phenomenon in the story but the result of a consistent narrative method.

In nonrealistic writing, stories derive their force not from resemblance to the known world but from their freedom from its constraints (cf. Licht, p. 124). The resolve of the heroes, the radical nature of their deeds, the rapidity of events, and the magnitude of the phenomena are what give the story its unambiguous clarity, one-time exclusivity, and dramatic power. In all of these respects, the Book of Jonah resembles the frame tale of the Book of Job. On the material plane, Job is "wealthier than anyone in the East" (1:3); on the spiritual plane, "there is no one like him on earth" (1:8; 2:3). Within a single day, he loses all his possessions to bandits and natural disasters—"God's fire" (1:16) and "a great wind" (1:19). The boils that infest him leave him no bit of skin uninflamed—"from the sole of his foot to the crown of his head" (2:7). Of equal magnitude with these catastrophes is the extreme nature of the challenge of his wife, who is certain that he would be better off dead and urges him to "blaspheme God and die!" (2:9). Typological numbers, which express quantitative wholeness, are used to designate the size of his family (1:2), the amplitude of his possessions (1:3), and the duration of the days of his consolation (2:13). In the story of Jonah, too, everything (except for the incident of the plant) is impressively large: "a great wind" (1:4) causes "a great storm" (1:4); "The men feared greatly" (1:10) leads to "The men feared the LORD greatly" (1:16); "a great fish" (2:1) swallows Jonah, and "a great city to God" (1:2; 3:2, 3; 4:11) responds to his call; the clemency shown to Nineveh causes him to be "displeased . . . greatly" (4:1), and the heaven-sent plant causes him "great joy" (4:6). The story begins with two unique events that have no parallel in other prophetic stories: the dispatch of a prophet of the Lord to proclaim imminent punishment to a gentile city, and the prophet's adamant refusal to perform his mission—to the point of preferring death. Here too, typological numbers are used to exaggerate the size of the city (3:3) and its population (4:11) and to emphasize the length of his stay in the belly of the fish (2:1) and of the stay of execution granted to the people of Nineveh (3:4). Here too, the magnitude of a deed is dramatized by the contraction of its duration to "one day" (3:4) and the emphasis on its completeness—"great and small alike" (3:5).

Despite this similarity in narrative method, it was not until the eighteenth century that anyone thought to say about Jonah what one of the talmudic sages said about Job: "Job never existed, but was a parable" (B. Baba Batra 15a). On the contrary, Jonah's adventure is referred to as a historical event in the apocryphal books of Tobias (14:4 [short version only]) and 3 Maccabees (6:8), in Josephus (*Antiquities of the Jews* 9,10,2), and in M. Ta'anit (2,4): "May He who answered Jonah in the belly of the fish answer you and hearken to the voice of your crying this day." The members of the Maimonidean school, too, who had no qualms about denying the reality of the miracle of the fish (see above), did not consider the book as a whole to be a fiction, probably because historical and literary criteria did not concern them, or perhaps because they were afraid that doing so might serve as a precedent for other prophetic books (Tanhum ha-Yerushalmi, p. 108). For us, however, a literary investigation of the book is an essential tool for understanding it, without which we cannot hear everything it has to tell us.

An inquiry into the literary genre of the story must take account, in addition to its nonrealistic mode of composition, of everything else that distinguishes Jonah from the other prophetic books and their genres. The story of Jonah is full of miracles, but the prophet is always their object, never their initiator (Rofé, p. 135). Jonah is assigned a prophetic mission, but only two verses are devoted to its execution (3:3–4); the balance of the book recounts his fierce opposition to his mission, both before and after he performs it. The Ninevites' repentance is not described as a painful crisis but as a rapid reversal without second thoughts, thereby focusing our attention not on their contrition but on the prophet's anguished protest against its acceptance. Nor are the miracles described in a detailed and realistic fashion that might inspire readers with awe at the presence of the Lord and His mighty deeds or with astonishment at the capability of the man of God or recognition of his limitations. The narrator merely reports the miracles with dry factuality as overt and direct acts of God ("He appointed"), as His steps to counter Jonah's internal and external flight.

Thus the Book of Jonah is constructed from the same thematic building blocks as many other prophetic stories, but with one essential difference: every element has been transformed from a narrative motif to an object of inquiry, questioning and contemplation, and reaffirmation. This means that the Book of Jonah is to be located in the area between prophetic stories and the frame tale of Job. Like the former, it deals with a prophet and prophecy, with miracles and repentance; but like the frame tale of Job, it elucidates, in bold lines and stark colors, a fundamental issue in the relations between human beings and their Creator. We ought then to classify it as a "theological prophetic story," a description preferable to the closely related category of "*mašal* in the form of an example story" (Landes, p. 148) or "parable" (Rofé, p. 159), because the story and its lesson form a seamless whole with no external moral and because it does not depict Jonah as a "proverb and a byword" (Deut. 28:37) and a negative exemplum (just as Job is not presented as a positive character for emulation). More than they are supposed to judge the personality of the desperate fugitive, who is at once bold and stubborn, upright and ludicrous, readers are called upon to observe the series of surprises that the Lord has in store for His prophet, who had the audacity to claim to know how to conduct His world better than its Creator does.

Ironic Satire or Compassionate Irony? There is a widespread view that Jonah is a profoundly humorous book, though generations of readers failed to appreciate this because of their great reverence for the sacred writings. Such restraint is not justified, however, given that humor is not necessarily the same thing as irreverent jesting. On the contrary, ironic satire can lay painfully bare the disparity between Jonah's self-image and his true nature and deride his erroneous ideas in the mirror of the absurd situations in which he finds himself. According to this view, nothing is more ridiculous than a prophet who tries to run away from God (whose dominion over sea and land he evidently acknowledges), who sleeps soundly while the ship is in danger of foundering, and who must be summoned to pray to his God by the pagan captain. Moreover, there is delicious irony in God's frustration with Jonah's plans: the man who tries to run away from his prophetic vocation unintentionally increases the gentile sailors' reverence for the Lord; the man who flees from his God toward death must eventually call to him, even against his will, from the belly of a fish. How ludicrous is this man who tries to run away to Tarshish in the hold of a ship and is returned to dry land in the belly of a fish! How humiliating is it for him to be swallowed by a fish and, even more so, to be vomited forth from its mouth. The proponents of this view are astounded by the double standard of the prophet, who can utter a psalm of thanksgiving to God for rescuing him from drowning but has no qualms about protesting the salvation of Nineveh. The contradiction reaches its zenith in the rapid turnabout from "This was a *great* evil to Jonah" (after the reprieve granted to the city) to his "*great* joy" (over the growth of the plant), which is so quickly rescinded (when the plant withers and dies). We are also supposed to laugh out loud at the thought of beasts clothed in sackcloth, bawling to God because they have been deprived of food and water; to nod our heads at the ironic contrast between the gentile city's response to the call of the foreign prophet and Jerusalem's refusal to heed Jeremiah's warning (chapter 36); and to smile when we read Jonah's plea for death after his astounding success in Nineveh, recognizing it as a close parody of Elijah's similar plea after his *failure* in Jezreel.

These illustrations of the humorous nature of Jonah, which are generally advanced in isolation from an overall conception of the book, shall be considered here in light of our own reading of the story. Most of these points receive a different explanation in the body of the commentary; here we need consider only the most important ones. First and foremost, the moral grandeur of the man who could say, "Lift me and cast me into the sea" (1:12), should warn us against condescending scorn. The fundamental seriousness of the fugitive prophet and his utter fidelity to himself are meant to arouse the reader's sympathy rather than derision: Jonah is a genuinely pathetic figure in his hopeless struggle with his God. True, there is no shortage of irony in a situation where the prophet of the Lord refrains from joining his prayer to those of the sailors; but this silence, as the fruit of a serious crisis of faith and the logical conclusion of his repudiation of his prophetic vocation, is not absurd at all. On the contrary, the irony actually intensifies the pathos. Making your home in a fish's abdomen may not be a particularly dignified experience, but the embarrassment is mitigated by the fact that being swallowed saves Jonah from drowning and being vomited onto dry land releases him from his confinement. The allegation that Jonah is guilty of a double standard itself suffers from moral insensitivity: however grave the sin of his flight, one can hardly demand that he place himself on the level of the wicked people of the city. Again, the reading of Nineveh's repentance as a taunting retort to the rejectionism of Jerusalem quite ignores the fact that the overt idealization of what takes place in Nineveh in a single day invalidates any contrast with what may realistically be expected of the historical Jerusalem (the possible literary links with Jeremiah, chapter 36, are discussed under "The Book of Jonah and the Book of Jeremiah: Influence without Contrast," p. xxxix). And whether the inclusion of the beasts in the fasting and sackcloth contributes to the idealization of the city's repentance, or makes it absurd (see Comment to 3:7–8), it is clear that either view is incompatible with taking the Ninevites' repentance as satirical criticism of the intransigence of Israel.

The Book of Jonah, then, is not an ironic satire. Furthermore, what irony it does contain is not particularly biting. It looks down on the hero and painfully exposes his failures, but it is forgiving: It sets the hero in his proper place without humiliating him and restores him to his dignity without abasing him. Jonah permits himself to defy the Lord's command and holds fast to his opposition even after being compelled to execute it, all on account of his unwavering fidelity to strict justice and his foreknowledge that the Lord will indeed repent of His fatal intent. He suffers from self-righteousness and conceit; these are the traits of which the divine irony comes to wean him. His know-it-all hubris is satirized by a plot that is full of surprises: his flight is interrupted by the storm, his drowning is prevented by the fish, his stay in the fish is protracted, and the plant grows up overnight and withers overnight. His self-righteousness is satirized by the juxtaposition of the prophet's stubbornness against the submissiveness of the gentile sailors and the people of Nineveh. By means of unexpected events and less-than-flattering contrasts, the Lord makes it plain, in the language of action that is stronger than any speech, that the duty to obey applies even to those who are righteous in their own eyes; moreover, that the gates of prayer and repentance are open even to one who goes so far astray as to deem God's responsivness to be a divine flaw and His forbearance a weakness. Jonah comes to realize that sinners' love of life is not just a failing; it leads them astray, but it also leads them to repentance. He also discovers that his own zeal for justice is not only a merit; just as it leads him to self-control and adherence to the law, it also leads him to self-negation and to flouting a divine injunction. The merciful irony that undercuts his conceit and righteousness leads Jonah to recognize the heavy but loving hand of the Lord, who wishes to return him, too, to His bosom.

The Narrative Art

Why Is the Motive of Jonah's Flight Concealed until Chapter 4?

Jonah is not the only one who fails to explain his flight with a statement of justification or challenge; the narrator is an accomplice in this silence. This total concealment of the hero's motives until the end of the story (a temporary gap) is unique in the corpus of biblical stories and makes it difficult to be satisfied with the conventional answer that its purpose is to increase the suspense. Sternberg (pp. 318–320) offers the opposite answer: Jonah is not a thriller whose readers are aware of a problem and tensely anticipate its resolution. It is a story of surprise, whose readers think they understand the hero and his motives—only to find out, to their astonishment, that they have been misled. He maintains that we are not supposed to notice the silence about Jonah's motive because we think it self-evident: the prophet is too kindhearted to inform the great city of its imminent destruction; his flight is a protest against the wrathful God. Our sympathy for him is heightened when he advises the sailors to cast him into the sea, even as the image of the Lord as a vengeful deity is reinforced by His merciless pursuit of the fugitive prophet. Then, without warning, everything is turned upside down in the fourth chapter, when Jonah explicitly says that he ran away out of concern for his reputation as an authentic prophet, and we discover that the Lord has forgone His own honor to facilitate the return of transgressors.

It seems to us, however, that softheartedness does not easily go together with bold remonstration; furthermore, the two ostensible motives—Jonah's and the Lord's—are far from obvious (see Tribble, p. 203). It is equally, if not more plausible, that readers understand Jonah's categorical refusal to prophesy against Nineveh and his willingness to pay the full price for this dereliction as motivated by his belief that the corrupt city of Nineveh does not deserve a warning of its impending doom and a last chance to repent. The prophet's flight is a revolutionary and astonishing act that demands an immediate explanation. The narrator's conspicuous silence arouses readers' strong curiosity about the hero's unstated motives and causes one to wonder why this information is being withheld.

Jonah's silence is part of his defiance; just as he prays only out of compulsion, so too he does not address the Lord in words until after the fact, when he is again overcome by despair. The narrator would not be violating the hero's silence by adopting language such as, "Jonah, however, arose to flee to Tarshish; for he said in his heart, 'I know that the LORD is a compassionate and gracious God, slow to anger, abounding in kindness, and repenting of evil.'" Had the narrator done so, the confrontation between divine justice and divine mercy would extend through the entire story, from its beginning until its end. The story as written, however, makes a clean separation between the Lord's pursuit of His prophet (chapters 1 and 2) and the theme of justice versus mercy (chapters 3 and 4). This division has two results, one for the fugitive and one for his pursuer.

Readers, well aware that they are facing a difficult riddle (which becomes more intriguing when they find that the feelings and motives of the other characters are presented in detail—1:5, 7, 10, 14, 16; 3:5, 9), wonder what momentous consideration impelled the prophet to his vain flight and hopeless rebellion. When the answer is finally supplied, in chapter 4, readers can ponder the legitimacy of the ethical position that informed Jonah's action after they have already been impressed by the vigor of his opposition and unbending earnestness. Recounting the fateful sequence of events before exploring the world view that motivated them gives this elucidation, when it comes, added existential depth, and intellectual validity: The forceful rejection of the doctrine of mercy is voiced by a man who was willing to die rather than cause others to die, and who was willing to leave his native land and pay with his life rather than serve the compassionate God. His vigorous and sincere opposition to divine mercy is striking evidence that it is desperately needed. Just as the flight is unqualified, so is the pursuit relentless. The Lord is not interested in Jonah's emotional distress and dismisses his ethical scruples. He blocks all avenues of flight and forces the prophet to approach Him in prayer and go in His name to Nineveh. Jonah must bow his head before the absolute sovereignty of the divine will—like the sailors, who say, "For You, O LORD, by Your will, have brought this about" (1:14)—before he can hear and understand the explanation given by God, who forgives without being lenient. The gates of escape are shut in the prophet's face; precisely this provides the opening of the gates of repentance to the transgressors with its full significance, since both are direct outcomes of the Lord's love for His creatures. The paradoxical tension between the Lord's inordinate severity with Jonah and His extraordinary leniency with Nineveh teaches us about the absolute sovereignty of the divine will; it is resolved only when Jonah comes to realize that the will of the Lord is not arbitrary, but compassionate, for those who are near and for those who are far from Him.

The Structure of the Story   In the Leningrad codex (which dates from 1009), which reflects the textual tradition of Ben Asher, there is a minor ("closed") section break after 2:10, a major ("open") break after 2:11, and another minor break after 4:3. A division more sensitive to the plot seems to have been prevalent in Spain, since five Spanish liturgical poets (Joseph ibn Avitur, Solomon ibn Gabirol, Isaac ibn Giat, Moses ibn Ezra, and Abraham ibn Ezra) each wrote a set of three poems based on the Book of Jonah for inclusion in the Reader's Repetition of the ʿ*Amidah* (specifically in the *Kedushah* section) of the Additional Service for the Day of Atonement; all reflect the following division: (1) 1:1–2:1 (the conclusion of chapter 1 in the Authorized Version as well); (2) 2:2–2:11; (3) 3:1–4:11. Abravanel divided the book into "prophecies" and "sections," as was his wont with the other prophetic books. The division into two "prophecies" corresponds to the bisection of the book by the open section break after 2:11. It is substantiated by the close parallel between the opening of the story (1:1–3), where the divine injunction and its violation are described, and the scene found in 3:1–3a, where the injunction is repeated and this time obeyed (see the detailed comparison in the introduction to vv. 3:1–3a, p. 25). The parallel between these two opening scenes is continued through the other scenes in the two halves of the story, giving the entire book a symmetrical structure:

Part 1: The flight and its failure	*Part 2: Rebellion and acquiescence*
1. The injunction and its violation (1:1–3)	1. The repeated injunction and its fulfillment (3:1–3a)
2. In the storm-tossed ship: the sailors' obedience and Jonah's rebellion (1:4–16)	2a. In Nineveh, the doomed: the sinners' repentance (3:3b–10)
	2b. In Nineveh, the forgiven: Jonah's second rebellion (4:1–5)
3. In the belly of the fish: submission (2:1–11)	3. East of Nineveh: acquiescence (4:6–11)

There is one striking difference. On the ship, Jonah's rebellion is interwoven with the account of the sailors' obedience. The parallel scene in the second half, set in Nineveh, is divided into two parts: the first is the repentance by the people of Nineveh, and the second is the prophet's second rebellion. This structural variation reflects the progress of the plot: in the first part, the prophet runs away to avoid fulfilling the divine injunction, whereas in the second part, having been compelled to implement it, he rebels against its outcome. Except for this change in the timing of his rebellion, however, the structures of the two parts are fundamentally similar. On the ship, Jonah prefers to be cast overboard rather than call upon his God; after Nineveh has been pardoned, he again prefers to die rather than acknowledge the righteousness of the Lord. And just as he initially attempted to avoid going to Nineveh, after he does go, he refuses to leave it and return to his own country. Instead he settles down east of the city in a desperate attempt to prove to God that *his* is the way of justice.

This view of Jonah's departure from Nineveh (4:5) as the active extension of his verbal protest leads to a twofold conclusion. Although many scholars do so, we cannot detach 4:5 from the Nineveh scene. Instead, we must read this verse as its conclusion (structurally parallel to Jonah's being cast into the sea). Thematic and formal confirmation of the symmetrical pattern and the consequent delineation of the scenes is provided by the striking resemblance between the opening lines of the scenes that conclude the two parts of the story. In the third scene of part 1 we read, "The LORD appointed a great fish to swallow Jonah" (2:1); correspondingly, in the third scene of part 2, "The LORD God appointed a ricinus plant, which grew up above Jonah, to provide shade over his head and save him from his distress" (4:6). Parallel to the fish, which saved him from drowning but became his prison for "three days and three nights," the plant is given to Jonah to "save him from his distress," only to be taken away from him "overnight."

All seven scenes of the story conclude with a pause that briefly halts the flow of the plot. Readers intuit the pause from the slowed pace of the story, created by means of redundant stylistic flourishes or by a return (stylistic or thematic) to the beginning of the scene, which creates an envelope structure or *inclusio.* The first scene ends with a stylistic device—the emphatic repetition of "Tarshish" three times in a single verse (1:3). The second scene concludes with an *inclusio,* in which the ending inverts the opening situation:

1:4–5

But the LORD *cast* a great wind upon the sea,

and...a great storm came upon the sea....

The sailors *were afraid* and cried out, each to *his own god*....

1:15–16

And they lifted Jonah and *cast* him into the sea,

and *the sea* stopped raging.

The men *feared the* LORD greatly....

The closing verse of this second scene (1:16) has another stylistic flourish—three successive internal accusatives (that is, nouns which stand as the object of a verb derived from the same stem—a frequent locution in Hebrew, but almost unknown in English except in such set phrases as "fight the good fight"). These flourishes give the verse a stately, even ceremonial nature. Literally translated, it reads: "The men feared the LORD a great fear; they sacrificed a sacrifice to the LORD and they vowed vows." Although the internal accusative is a normal stylistic feature of biblical Hebrew, only the third of those in this verse, "vowing a vow," is a standard idiom.

The third scene also concludes with an *inclusio* in which the end resolves the beginning:

2:1

The LORD appointed a great fish to swallow Jonah....

2:11

The LORD commanded the fish, and it spewed Jonah out upon dry land.

The fourth scene, however, concludes with an *inclusio* where the end is the emphatic fulfillment of the opening and is reinforced by a chiastic (ABBA) structure:

3:1–2a

The *word of the* LORD came to Jonah....

Arise and go to Nineveh,...

3:3a

Jonah *arose and went to Nineveh*

in accordance with the *word of the* LORD.

The fifth scene ends (3:10) with both a stylistic repetition and a thematic *inclusio*. The former is represented by the threefold repetition of forms of the verb "to do": "God saw what they *did*.... God repented the evil which He had said *to do* to them, and did not *do* it." The latter returns us to the opening situation by nullifying it: the proclamation of the impending destruction of Nineveh (3:4) is abrogated by the Lord's repenting "the evil which He had said to do to them" (3:10).

The sixth scene ends with the stylistic redundancy of a threefold repetition of the word "city" (4:5), and the seventh scene with a threefold emphasis on the large population of Nineveh, by means of wordplay on various derivatives of the Hebrew roots *r-b-b* in the forms "more than" *(harbeh)*, "myriad" *(ribbo)*, and "many" *(rabbah)*, augmented by a stylistic *inclusio* that links the end of the entire story with its beginning:

1:2	4:11
Arise and go to Nineveh,	And should I not care about Nineveh,
that great city....	that great city!...

This division of the book into seven scenes is not prevalent among scholars and commentators. One reason for the wide divergence of views about the structure of Jonah is the strong tendency to demarcate sections on the basis of chiastic (ABBA) or concentric (ABCBA) patterns. Many of these patterns, though, are not based on the wording of the verses but on tendentious characterizations of elements; they establish not thematic but formal links, such as alternation of the protagonist's speeches and the narrator's comments. For all that they seek to impress us with the formal sophistication of the story, they do not necessarily enhance our understanding of it. The patterns suggested for the second half of Jonah are much more forced than those proposed for the first half, evidently because of the desire to find them in every scene. However, the fact that the entire first scene cannot be fit into the sophisticated concentric structure proposed by Lohfink (p. 200) for 1:3 should inspire us to be wary of this tendency.

    A. Jonah, however, arose to flee to Tarshish from the presence of the Lord.
    B.   He went down to Joppa
    C.   and found a ship
    D.   going to Tarshish.
    C.   He paid the fare
    B.   and went down into it
    A. to go with the others to Tarshish, away from the presence of the Lord.

This striking architecture, which has won the approbation of so many, has two defects. First, the obvious syntactical resemblance (one or two verbs plus an infinitive) between the first and third sentences has been blurred for the sake of graphical symmetry. Second, the words at the center, "going to Tarshish," receive an inordinate weight that is hard to justify thematically. Better than this concentric pattern is a simpler one that is more faithful to the text while highlighting the threefold reference to Jonah's destination, which unites the five verbs and two infinitives into a single goal-oriented action:

    Jonah, however, arose to flee to Tarshish from the presence of the Lord. He went down to Joppa and found a ship going to Tarshish.
    He paid the fare and went down into it to go with the others to Tarshish, away from the presence of the Lord.

On the other hand, the second scene (1:4–16) does indeed have a concentric structure, as suggested by Lohfink (pp. 200–201) and with even greater sophistication by Pesch (pp. 578–579). Here we transcribe this structure using a literal rendering of the actual text, waiving the precise formal perfection in favor of a more accurate representation of the sequence of events (table 1). The chiastic reflection of the first half of the scene in the second half enriches the story by creating a web of associations (analogical, contrasting, and causal) that is woven, overtly and otherwise, between the parallel elements.

Table 1. The Structure of the Shipboard Scene (1:4–16)

The storm inspires fear	A	But the LORD *cast* a great wind upon *the sea*, and . . . a great storm came upon *the sea*. . . . The sailors *were afraid*. . . .
Vain prayer	B	The sailors . . . cried out, each to his own god. . . .
Vain efforts	C	They cast the ship's cargo into the sea *to make it lighter for them*.
Jonah pays no attention	D	But Jonah, meanwhile, went down into the hold of the vessel where he lay down and fell asleep.
Jonah is summoned to help	E	The captain . . . said to him, "*How can you be* sleeping so soundly! Arise and cry . . . and we will not perish."
Discovery of the culprit	F	"Let us cast lots that we *may know* on whose account this evil has come upon us." They cast lots and the lot fell on Jonah.
Questions to determine the nature of his crime	G	They said to him, "Tell us . . . *what* is your business? Where have you come from?"
Jonah's self-identification as one who fears the Lord magnifies their own fear		"I am a Hebrew," he replied. "I *fear* the LORD. . . ." The men *feared* greatly.
Reproving question	G'	They said to him, "*What* have you done!"
Flashback: the crime is already known to them	F'	For the men *knew* that he was fleeing from the presence of the LORD, for so he had told them.
Jonah is summoned to help	E'	Then they said to him, "*What* shall we do to you to make the sea calm around us?"
Jonah takes responsibility	D'	He answered, "Lift me and cast me . . . for I know that this great storm came upon you on my account."
Vain efforts	C'	Nevertheless, the men rowed hard *to regain the dry land,* but they could not. . . .
Genuine prayer	B'	Then they called out to the LORD: ". . . Do not let us perish on account of this man's life. . . ."
The end of the tempest leads to the fear of the Lord	A'	And they lifted Jonah and *cast* him into *the sea*, and the *sea* stopped raging. The men *feared* the LORD *greatly*. . . .
Conclusion: expressions of thanks		They offered a sacrifice to the Lord and they made vows.

Lohfink (p. 196, n. 37) also found a chiastic structure in the third scene (2:1–11), when it is read without the psalm (on the entire question of bracketing the psalm, see "The Unity of the Book and the Provenance of the Psalm," p. xxxv):

A	The Lord's action	A	The LORD appointed a great fish to swallow Jonah....
B	Its effect on Jonah	B	And *Jonah* was in ***the belly of the fish*** three days and three nights.
A'	Jonah's action	B'	*Jonah* prayed to the LORD his God from ***the belly of the fish***.
B'	The Lord's reaction	A'	The LORD commanded the fish, and it spewed Jonah out upon dry land.

From the perspective of the plot, the structure of this scene is indeed chiastic: its end is the total inversion of its beginning, and Jonah's prayer is a direct result of his imprisonment. From the perspective of the characters' activity, however, the parallel is not chiastic (ABBA) but repetitive (ABAB): first the Lord acts and Jonah is acted upon; then Jonah acts and the Lord reacts. The latent tension between these two structural principles enhances the unity of the short scene.

The symmetrical structure of the story as a whole highlights the formal and thematic links between the prophet's two manifestations of rebellion—the external flight that ends in submission and the internal flight that ends in acquiescence. This reciprocal relationship, which is one of the keys to the richness of the book, is reinforced by another structural principle. Whereas the two scenes in which Jonah is entrusted with his mission (1:1–3; 3:1–3a) are related to each other, the second and third scenes in the first part are linked not only to their parallels in the second part but to all the other scenes as well, by means of the nearly uniform paradigm common to all of them (table 2). This pattern is based on three main elements: (1) a great misfortune (genuine or otherwise) sent by the Lord, (2) an address to God in word and deed (or the demonstrative avoidance thereof), and (3) the Lord's response (absent, of course, when He is not addressed). This recurring pattern creates the relations and contrasts between the appropriate responses of the sailors and Ninevites to their afflictions and the problematic responses of the rebellious prophet. In the second part, everything is more intense: the Ninevites' repentance in comparison with the sailors' obedience to the injunction to cast Jonah into the raging waters, Jonah's desperate protest against the Lord's mercy in comparision with his silence aboard ship, and his repeated refusal to pray after the withering of the plant in comparison with his involuntary prayer from the belly of the fish. All the prayers that request rescue from death—by the sailors, by the sinful people of Nineveh, and by Jonah in the belly of the fish—are heard. But Jonah's repeated death wish is frustrated or rejected. Only at the end of the book does Jonah merit a response from the Lord, an explicit and detailed statement in which God explains His ways to him.

Table 2. The Common Structural Paradigm of Scenes 2 and 3 in Each Part

Scene / Elements	I-2		I-3	II-2a	II-2b	II-3
Characters	Sailors	Jonah	Jonah	Ninevites	Jonah	Jonah
God-sent distress	"the ship was in danger of breaking up"	the Lord pursues His prophet	the fish that rescued Jonah becomes his prison	"Forty days more, and Nineveh shall be overturned"	the Lord's mercy angers Jonah	the plant that provided Jonah with shade withers and the sun beats down on his head
Prayer (and action)	the sailors pray to the Lord (and cast Jonah into the sea)	Jonah refuses to pray to the Lord (and continues his flight, toward the sea and death)	Jonah submits and prays for deliverance	prayer to God (and return from injustice)	protest-prayer: "Now, LORD, take my life" (and continued rebellion: Jonah watches the city from the east)	the despairing rebel asks for death but does not pray
Divine response	"and the sea stopped raging"		"the LORD commanded the fish, and it spewed Jonah out"	"God repented the evil"		God elucidates His ways and brings Jonah to accept them

Style KEY WORDS   The root *t-w-l* in the *hif'il* (causative construction) occurs three times in the ship scene: in the exposition of the problem—"the LORD cast a great wind upon the sea" (1:4); in its failed resolution—"they cast the ship's cargo into the sea" (v. 5); and in its actual solution—"they lifted Jonah and cast him into the sea" (v. 15). Most other key words appear in more than one scene and highlight the relations between similar or contrasting situations. Thus we find that the same verbs are used to depict the prayers and fears of the sailors and of the people of Nineveh: in the vessel, "the sailors . . . cried out" (1:5), "and we will not perish" (1:6), "they called out" (1:14), and "do not let us perish" (1:14); in Nineveh, "they called a fast" (3:5), the king "had the word cried" (3:7), "call mightily to God" (3:8), and "so that we do not perish" (3:9). Similarly, the verb *minnah,* "appoint," links the four agents dispatched by the Lord to bar Jonah's flight: the fish (2:1), the plant (4:6), the worm (4:7), and the east wind (4:8). The verb *yada',* "know," juxtaposes the confident knowledge of the prophet aboard the ship ("for I know" [1:12]) and in Nineveh ("for I knew" [4:2]) with the sailors' desperate appeal for knowledge ("that we may know" [1:7], "for the men knew" [1:10]); the religious caution of the king of Nineveh ("who knows" [3:9]); and the ignorance that protects the children of the city from destruction ("who do not yet know" [4:11]). The key word *ra'ah,* "evil," used in two of its senses—sin and punishment—applies to the sailors ("this evil" [1:7, 8]) as well as to the Ninevites ("their wickedness" [1:2], "evil ways" [3:8, 10], "God repented of the evil" [3:10]). For Jonah it has, ironically, a third meaning—the sense of injustice ("This was a great evil to Jonah" [4:1]).

"THE GROWING PHRASE"   Magonet (pp. 31–33) coined the term "the growing phrase" for the repetition of a phrase in expanded form. This pattern is used to describe the increasing severity of the squall: from "a great storm came upon the sea" (1:4) to "the sea was growing more and more stormy" (1:11) and finally to "the sea was growing more and more stormy about them" (1:13). At the same time, the sailors' emotional response progresses from "The sailors were afraid" (1:5) to "The men feared greatly" (1:10) and finally to "The men feared the LORD greatly" (1:16). Such expansion is also found in the repeated characterization of static elements: "that great city" (1:2; 3:2), "a great city to God" (3:3), and finally, "that great city, in which there are more than twelve myriad persons" (4:11). The device is also used ironically. After He pardons Nineveh, the Lord asks Jonah, "Are you that deeply angry?" (4:4). After the plant is blighted, He repeats the question, with an addition that is actually a diminution: "Are you so deeply angry about the plant?" (4:9). Jonah, oblivious to the irony, answers in the same words with an expansion he means as an intensification: "so deeply that I want to die" (4:9). The same device is also found in the frame tale of Job (for example, in the threefold repetition of Job's praises [1:1; 1:8; and 2:3])—another example of the generic similarity between these two stories (see "The Literary Genre," p. xvii).

WORDPLAY In the description of the growth of the plant, the play on *ẓel,* "shadow," and *le-haẓẓil,* "to save," is intensified by the frequent repetition of the *l* sound: *va-ya'aL me-'aL Le-yonah Li-hyot ẓeL 'aL rosho Le-haẓẓiL Lo me-ra'ato* (4:6). It may not be coincidental that there is wordplay in the other verses of "appointment," too: *dag gadol* "a great fish" (2:1), *tola'at ba'alot* ("a worm at dawn" (4:7)), *ruah harishit* ("a quiet... wind" [4:8]). We also encounter it in the verse that recounts the Lord's action on the sea: *hishevah le-hishaver* ("was in danger of breaking up" (1:4)). In his flight from the Lord, Jonah "went down" three times (twice in 1:3 and in 1:5); and it seems likely that *yarad,* "went down," is intentionally hidden in his fourth descent— into the depths of sleep (*va-yeradam,* "and fell asleep" [1:5]). (The "down" of "lay down" in the same verse is an artifact of translation only.) The wordplay on derivatives of the root *q-d-m* links *qiddamti li-vroah,* "I hastened to flee" (4:2), which refers to Jonah's first insubordination, with *mi-qedem la-'ir,* "east of the city" (4:5), which refers to his second, and both of them with *ruah qadim,* "east wind" (4:8), which, like the wind cast on the sea, is meant to return the fugitive to his God.

The Literary Function of the Gentiles as Supporting Characters

The two groups of gentiles play a large and essential role in the story, but their status is that of supporting characters who are of interest only by virtue of their relations with the hero. Structural proof of this is the fact that in the two scenes where they appear as a collective character, the narrator tells about them first, so that their actions can serve as a contrasting background to those of Jonah. We are then told how their problem was resolved, which suffices to send them back offstage. The description of what befalls Jonah, however, is deferred, and his predicament remains unresolved at the end of these scenes. Thus at the beginning of the ship scene we learn that Jonah has been sleeping belowdecks only after the vigorous activity of the sailors has been described, even though the two are simultaneous. At the end of this scene, the narrator calmly describes what the sailors did after the storm abated, leaving the fate of the prophet for the next scene.

In the second part of the story, this tactic is carried to the point of a division of the action into two discrete scenes. The repentance of the people of Nineveh and the abrogation of the decree against them are recounted to the very end, while nothing is said about what the prophet did in the city after delivering his message or about the circumstances and timing of his leaving it. His harsh reaction to the clemency shown the city is delayed to the next scene, in which the people of Nineveh do not play a part.

The structural proof is buttressed by a thematic one. The gentiles' compliance with the will of the Lord is so spontaneous and unproblematic, and the vacillations of the insubordinate prophet so severe and multifaceted, that it is perfectly clear that the former cannot be the linchpin of the story. Almost all readers of this book have within them something of the evil inclination of Jonah son of Amittai. But no one is truly disturbed by these exemplary gentiles who are too good to be true (see "The Literary Genre," p. xvii).

The inescapable question here is why these supporting characters are so emphatically described as gentiles. According to Bickerman (p. 43), Jonah was sent to distant Nineveh in order to show that the Lord has compassion and shows mercy even to the worst of sinners. His answer fails to explain, however, how the gentile sailors serve the objective of giving the book universal validity. On the other hand, we may cite Kaufmann's persuasive answer (p. 283) that the Book of Jonah—like the Sodom pericope (Genesis 19), the frame tale of Job, the wisdom chapters in Psalms, the Books of Proverbs and Ecclesiastes, and Ezekiel 14:12–23—is one of the ethical tracts of the Bible that pose their questions against a non-Israelite background. Because the Book of Jonah deals with a fundamental theological problem that has no specifically Israelite aspect, it is set in an ahistoric frame and among Noahides. Unlike the Book of Job, however, the hero of the Book of Jonah is a prophet of the Lord; there is a certain tension between the fact that Jonah is a Hebrew (1:9) and the other characters gentiles. That they are gentiles casts the embarrassment of the Hebrew hero who is fleeing from the Lord into greater relief (cf. Judg. 19:12; 1 Sam. 22:16–19; 2 Kings 5:8; Jer. 2:10–11; and Mal. 1:11). The sailors' fear and the Ninevites' repentance provide an ironic perspective on the prophet's flight and disapproval of divine mercy, while the bare existence of the masses who cannot distinguish their right hand from their left hand serves as a fit object for gratuitous compassion and mercy.

The Unity of the Book and the Provenance of the Psalm

Two cruxes have inspired doubts as to whether the last scene (4:6–11) was originally part of the book: the duplication of the shade provided by the booth (4:5) by the seemingly superfluous shade provided by the plant (4:6), and the alternating forms of the Divine Name, which can be explained elsewhere in the story but not here (see Comment to 4:6). The attempts to resolve these difficulties by distinguishing different sources of the book—attempts which also rely on the fact that the question "Are you that deeply angry?" is posed twice (4:4 and 4:9)—do not remove the difficulty because they do not provide an adequate explanation of the unexpected use of different Divine Names in this scene. Even most proponents of various conjectures about the composition of the book share the prevailing consensus that the Book of Jonah as we have it should be considered a single literary unity, except perhaps for Jonah's psalm (2:2–10).

In the introduction to chapter 2 (pp. 15–18), the main points of friction between the psalm and the body of the story are considered and a hypothesis is offered as to the motives for its later incorporation into the text. Here we shall briefly survey the various solutions advanced by those who believe that it has always occupied its present position. In fact, these forced glosses would seem, rather, to constitute additional proof of the severity of the problems they seek to resolve.

Daniel al-Kumissi said simply: "Then he prayed to the Lord after three days and nights: 'Save me!' And He saved him then." Because it is difficult to assume that the words "Save me" are intended to summarize the psalm, which omits any request for deliverance, al-Kumissi may have intended them as a gloss on the verb "prayed" (2:2), which he understood to refer to an unquoted supplication that preceded the song of thanksgiving, rather than to the psalm. Rashi, by contrast, viewed the psalm itself as a prayer for deliverance; he reads "From the belly of Sheol I cried out" (2:3) as referring not to Jonah's being swallowed up by the billows but to his present affliction—"from the belly of the fish, which is like Sheol to me"—and what follows as a flashback to his near-drowning in the sea.

Abraham ibn Ezra, in his commentary on 2:2, cited the audacious solution proposed by unnamed exegetes (evidently of the Spanish *peshat* school) who were sensitive enough to realize that the past-tense verbs in the psalm mean that it is a song of thanksgiving for a boon already granted. They were accordingly forced to gloss "from the belly of the fish" as meaning "*after* he had been spewed forth from the belly of the fish." Ibn Ezra dismissed this radical use of the rhetorical device of concision and the narrative principle that "there is no chronological order in Scripture" and returned to the view that the psalm is really a call for rescue. As a first-rate philologist, however, Ibn Ezra could not ignore the past tenses and was forced to say that as a prophetic prayer, uttered "with the holy spirit and prophetic spirit," it combines a genuine prayer for deliverance from the belly of the fish with an immediate awareness of the anticipated response—expressed in what is known today as the "prophetic past" (past in form, future in signification).

Because some contemporary scholars rely on Ibn Ezra here, we should realize how problematic he himself found this reading of Jonah's psalm. Evidence of this is the lyrical paraphrase of 2:3, which he incorporates into a liturgical poem (*piyyut*) for the Day of Atonement, based on Jonah's prayer. As a poet, exempt from the restrictions that bind the exegete, he takes over the verb "I called" in its original form but converts "and He answered me" to an imperative and replaces "I cried out" and "You heard" with verbs in the future tense: "Lofty One, Eternal Life, I called to You—answer me!/I was buried in the mouth of the living [i.e., the belly of the fish]—restore my life/and from the depths of the earth, raise me up again!" (*Sacred Poems II,* ed. Y. Levin [Jerusalem, 1970], p. 79 [Heb.]). In *Midrash Jonah,* too, the prophet is assigned a long prayer that begins with recognition of the impossibility of running away from the Lord of All and ends with a plea for deliverance, in the imperative and optative moods (the latter has the form of a future tense in Hebrew): "Please answer me from the belly of She'ol, and save me from the depths. And may my prayer come before you, and speedily perform my request" (ed. Jellinek, p. 99).

Abravanel demurred at Ibn Ezra's overly sophisticated solution: "To me there seems to be no need for the remark of R. Abraham ibn Ezra, which is good and correct in itself, because in this prayer there is no past tense in place of a future." He offered instead a much more daring solution, based on acceptance as biographical fact of the midrashic identification of Jonah with the son of the widow from Zarephath: "'I cried out, and You heard my voice': Here he alluded to the miracle worked for him in the time of Elijah, who restored his life after he had died; it is about that episode that he says here, 'I called . . . I cried out'—all in the past tense. This does not mean that he actually called and cried out, but is rather a metaphoric reference to that [earlier] miracle."

Some, who detect a thick layer of irony and satire in the book, attempt to maintain the thanksgiving psalm as given but claim that it is meant as a supplication: Jonah believes that expressing thanks for his preservation from drowning is all that is needed to move God to restore him to dry land. Only readers sense the disparity between what he finally says to the Lord and what he should have said (Magonet, pp. 52–53; Ackerman). Another group—those who believe that the recitation of a psalm of thanksgiving is appropriate to Jonah's situation in the fish—must argue that he does not feel the fish as a dark dungeon in which he has spent three days and three nights with no hope of escape, but as his savior from drowning, which rescued him from the bottom of the sea, or the underworld, which—according to Sumerian tradition—is a three days' journey from dry land (Landes, pp. 11–13). Not only is this understanding of the Sumerian parallel controversial and its application to biblical cosmography extremely doubtful, but the text itself seems incompatible with it: If it takes three days to return from the underworld, the same period of time is required to reach it. Why doesn't the narrator tell readers how Jonah survived such a protracted period under water?

But more is missing from the psalm than a request for deliverance; absent, too, are confession and an appeal for forgiveness. Evidence of how deeply this troubles readers is provided by the free paraphrases of the psalm in the *Antiquities of the Jews* ("And he asked God to forgive his sins" [9,10,2]), in the Koran ("I was indeed one of the sinners" [Sura 21:87–88]), and especially in the Sephardi liturgical poems for the Day of Atonement (for example, the aforementioned hymn by Abraham ibn Ezra: "In truth, who has hardened his heart to Him and has remained whole?/When I fled, He set me in the heart of the sea, hidden;/He made me dwell in darkness like those long dead").

All these exegetical dilemmas and problems indicate how difficult it is to insist that the psalm is an original part of the story. A similar case is the prayer of Hannah (1 Sam. 2:1–10), which does not fit well into the story of Samuel's birth. Moreover, there are three formal proofs that poetic prayers were incorporated into stories in places where later generations felt their lack: (1) Hezekiah's thanksgiving prayer is found in Isa. 38:9–20 but not in the parallel narrative in 2 Kings 20:2. (2) The prayer of Azariah and the thanksgiving psalm of the three friends who were saved from the fiery furnace were added to the Septuagint text of Daniel 3 between verses 23 and 24. (3) The prayers of Mordecai and Esther were added to the Septuagint version of Esther after 4:17. Thus nothing impedes our assuming that a prayer of thanksgiving for his deliverance from drowning was added to the story of Jonah, as a poetic expansion of an original "then Jonah prayed . . . from the belly of the fish." (Without the psalm, the scene has a clear structure: see "The Structure of the Story," p. xxvi.)

Links between Jonah and Other Biblical Books

The image of the recalcitrant prophet is etched in a contrasting relationship to his predecessors. To make readers aware of these contrasts, the narrator employs various expressions used in other stories to describe similar circumstances. In the body of the commentary, we have noted and commented on anti-correspondences between Jonah and Abraham (see 4:5) and between Jonah and Elijah (see 1:1; 1:3; 1:5; 1:6; and 4:3). Here we shall discuss the identification of Jonah with the prophet from Gath-hepher and three other intertextual links.

The Identification of Jonah with the Prophet Who Brought Good Tidings to Sinful Israel　The first verse of the book clearly identifies its hero with the prophet Jonah son of Amittai, who, according to 2 Kings 14:25–27, prophesied that King Jeroboam II, although a sinner who also caused the people to sin, would restore the northern frontier of Israel to the border of David and Solomon (1 Kings 8:65). The significance of this identification is not made explicit; any conjecture about it results from how one understands the story in the first place. Those who hold that Jonah was motivated by his concern for his credibility as a prophet see his identification with the prophet whose promise to Jeroboam was fulfilled as biographical support for his own erroneous expectation that this message would be realized as well. On the other hand, those who believe that Jonah fled to Tarshish because of his fierce opposition to the extension of the Lord's mercy and goodness to all His creatures maintain that this exclusivism is appropriate for a nationalistic court prophet who foresees good fortune for Israel and triumphs for its king. A weighty objection to this prevalent view has already been advanced, namely, that Jonah son of Amittai is not described in 2 Kings 14:25–27 as a false prophet but as a faithful messenger who conveys the word of the Lord as spoken to him ("in accordance with the promise that the LORD, the God of Israel, had made through His servant, the prophet Jonah son of Amittai"). Furthermore, the text in Kings goes on to explain that the Lord delivered Israel through the person of the sinful Jeroboam because He saw its political and military abasement and because the time for its destruction had not yet arrived ("For the LORD saw the very bitter plight of Israel . . . with none to help Israel. And the LORD resolved not to blot out the name of Israel from under heaven; and He delivered them through Jeroboam son of Joash"). That, too, is a case of the Lord's mercy overcoming strict justice, though not because the sinners have repented and not because they are the Lord's creatures. The reason is, rather, that the Lord has mercy on the weak and is forbearing with the wicked.

According to the first two opinions, the Book of Jonah must describe a later stage in the prophet's life than that recounted in 2 Kings 14. For those who view Jonah as a prophet zealous for strict divine justice, his eponymous book is a sort of consecration story, in which his mission to Nineveh prepares him for his second mission—bringing good tidings to those who have not and will not repent.

Jonah and Moses: Flight and Protest versus Intervention and Advocacy   There is a fundamental analogy between the overthrow decreed for Nineveh and the sentence of total destruction passed upon Israel after the sin of the Golden Calf (Exod. 32:10). Yet readers seem to be unaware of this similarity until they realize that the king's decree to the people of Nineveh, "Who knows, God may turn and repent, and turn back from His wrath, so that we do not perish" (3:9), echoes Moses's prayer on behalf of his people, "Turn back from Your wrath, and repent of the evil to Your people" (Exod. 32:12), while the narrator's comment that "God repented the evil which He had said to do to them, and did not do it" (3:10) echoes the acceptance of Moses's entreaty, "the LORD repented of the evil which He had said to do to His people" (Exod. 32:14).

Not only does Jonah leave it for the gentile king to enunciate what a prophet might be expected to say, but the contrast between him and Moses is made even stronger after the fact. Moses asked the Lord, "pray let me know Your ways, that I may know You" (Exod. 33:13), and was met by the veiled presence of the Lord, preceded by the announcement that His bounty cannot be foreseen: "I will grant grace that I will grant, and show the compassion that I will show" (v. 19). Later, when he climbed to the top of Mount Sinai, the Lord made His attributes known to him and Moses hastened to prostrate himself on the ground (34:5–8). Jonah, by contrast, asserts that the ways of the Lord are already known to him, "For I knew that You are a compassionate and gracious God, slow to anger, . . ." (4:2). He reproves Heaven by stating that he does not consider the divine attribute of mercy to be praiseworthy. He even expects that he will soon be shown to have been right, and God mistaken (see Comment to 4:5).

These contrasts with Moses are so obvious that we must allow that not only are we and the narrator aware of them, Jonah is too. This means that, in addition to fleeing the particular mission to Nineveh, Jonah also rebelled against the prophet's dual role— speaking in the Lord's name to human beings, and speaking to the Lord in their name and on their behalf. The Lord's response is designed to help him abandon his smug certainty and achieve true knowledge, to end his flight from God and man and seek closeness and contact, and to understand that the Lord spares the people of Nineveh because they are His creatures, just as He spared the Israelites because they are His people whom he brought out of Egypt (Exod. 32:11–14).

The Book of Jonah and the Book of Jeremiah: Influence without Contrast   There is much to recommend the view that the repentance of Nineveh described in chapter 3 is a narrative embodiment of the doctrine of repentance phrased as an abstract principle in Jer. 18:7–8: "At one moment I may decree that a nation or a kingdom shall be uprooted and pulled down and destroyed; but if that nation against which I made the decree turns back from its wickedness, I change My mind concerning the punishment I planned to bring on it."

An even stronger association—both thematic and linguistic—exists between Jonah 3 and Jeremiah 36, where the Lord enjoins Jeremiah to write down all the prophecies he has delivered over the last twenty-three years and expresses the hope that "*perhaps* when the House of Judah hear of all the disasters I intend to bring upon them, they will *turn back every one from his evil ways,* and I will pardon their iniquity and their sin" (v. 3). Baruch son of Neriah read the words of the Lord from the scroll on a public fast day in one of the chambers of the House of the Lord, "to all the people" (v. 10). The people's response is not reported, but "all the officials" (v. 14.) who heard a second reading of the scroll "turned to each other in fear" (v. 16). After verifying that the scroll contained a faithful record of all Jeremiah's prophecies, they advised Baruch and Jeremiah to hide from the wrath of King Jehoiakim and brought the matter to the monarch's attention. The scroll was then read to the king of Judah, who "was sitting in the winter house" (v. 22). "The king and all his courtiers who heard all these words showed no fear and did not tear their garments" (v. 24); what is more, as the reading proceeded, the scroll itself was tossed, section by section, into the fire. Then the king ordered the arrest of Baruch and Jeremiah. The Lord, however, hid His prophet, commanded him to write another scroll, which, like its predecessor, would include the prophecy of the destruction of Judah: "the king of Babylon will come and destroy this land and cause *man and beast* to cease from it" (v. 29). The gates of repentance, which king and courtiers failed to enter, were now sealed shut.

We find the exact opposite of this sequence of events in the nonrealistic account of Jonah's prophecy in Nineveh. All the people of the city, "great and small alike" (3:5), believe in the brief (five words in Hebrew) prophecy of doom, which only a third of them have heard directly, and quickly proclaim a fast and don sackcloth. The king, too, who hears the rumor at second hand, responds at once, without an attempt to verify its credibility: "he rose from his throne, took off his robe, put on sackcloth, and sat in ashes" (v. 6). Then "the king and his nobles" enjoined *"man and beast"* (v. 7) to fast and put on sackcloth and cry mightily to God, and ordered every person to *"turn back from his evil ways"* (v. 8) because there is still hope: *"Who knows,* God may turn and repent, and turn back from His wrath, so that we do not perish" (v. 9). Their return is indeed accepted.

This contrastive parallelism demands comment. For the universalist interpretation, which reads the Book of Jonah as directed against Jewish exclusivism, the parallel has a clear objective: criticizing Jerusalem by contrasting it with Nineveh, thereby providing hope that all mankind may attain faith (Wolff, p. 146). If this had been the author's intention, however, the repentance of Nineveh would have been given greater verisimilitude by means of a more realistic account, and Jerusalem and Israel would have been directly introduced into the story in some fashion, not through a countertext that only alert readers would pick up. What is more, the chronological assignment of Jonah to the age of Jeroboam II prevents the narrator from using Jeremiah's failure as a contrasting background to Jonah's success, which preceded it by more than 150 years. Thus it is more plausible to assume that because the repentance of Nineveh is fictional and hypothetical (and its completeness a direct result of its unreality) and intended to provide a backdrop for an inquiry into the prophet's principled opposition to divine leniency, it could be structured as the converse of the somber story in Jeremiah 36. There is certainly a strong literary influence, but there is no intentional contrast.

Echoes of the Prophet Joel in the Words of the King of Nineveh   Joel 1–2 describes the imminent arrival of swarms of locusts, the great host of the Lord that will do His will and consume all the produce of the field. The prophet for his part calls on the Lord to have mercy on the beasts who have no pasturage (1:19–20). In the name of the Lord he calls on Israel to repent, in the hope that the evil can still be averted: "'Turn back to Me with all your hearts, and with fasting, weeping, and lamenting.' Rend your hearts rather than your garments, and turn back to the LORD your God. For He is gracious and compassionate, slow to anger, abounding in kindness, and *repenting of evil. Who knows* but He may turn and repent? . . . " (2:12–14). In Nineveh, the mere proclamation of the impending doom was enough to bring commoners and king to do just what Joel tried to get the people of Judah to do by enumerating the attributes of mercy (precisely as they are listed and censured by Jonah). Because it is unthinkable that opprobrium was reused for praise, it follows either that the two stories have a common origin or that Jonah consciously echoes Joel. But in light of the conjectured assignation of the prophet Joel to the Second Temple period, it is most unlikely that the author of the Book of Jonah would attempt to make the ancient prophet appear ludicrous by means of a contrast with the later prophet. We are left to conclude that Joel's prophecy (like Jeremiah 36) was inverted to help depict immediate compliance with the word of the Lord, whose fullness provides an appropriate background for Jonah's moral opposition to its acceptance by the Lord.

Language

While the Book of Jonah is written in the same classical biblical Hebrew as the pre-exilic books, it also contains an appreciable accretion of linguistic phenomena that belong to later biblical Hebrew. Their lateness is attested by their presence in books written after the destruction of the First Temple and their prevalence in Aramaic, the Hebrew of the Dead Sea Scrolls, and Mishnaic Hebrew. The list that follows includes only those cases about which there is a broad consensus in the scholarly works listed in the bibliography.

Vocabulary

"Give us a thought" (1:6): *yit'ashet* from the Aramaic root *'-sh-t* (Dan. 6:4), instead of the classical Hebrew verb *ḥ-sh-b,* which has this meaning in Ps. 40:18.

"[Will become] calm" (1:11, 12): *yishtoq,* standard in Aramaic and Mishnaic Hebrew, is found here, in Ps. 107:30, and in Prov. 26:20, instead of the older *yaḥarish.*

"Raging" (lit. "its rage"–1:15): *za'po.* The noun *za'af* with the meaning "storm" is found in the Dead Sea Scrolls and Aramaic, but this is its only occurrence in the Bible (in Ps. 11:6 we find the derivative form *zil'afot,* "scorching").

[He] "appointed" (2:1 and 4:6, 7, 8): *va-yeman.* The root *m-n-h* with the sense of "appoint" or "entrust" and in the *pi'el* (intensive construction) is found only in Job,

Daniel, and Chronicles, as well as in Aramaic and Mishnaic Hebrew. In the older books we find *hifqid* (e.g., Lev. 26:16).

"A walk" (3:3, 4): *mahalakh*. With the meaning of "distance" and in place of the older *derekh* (Gen. 30:36; Exod. 3:18), found only here and in Neh. 2:6, as well as in Aramaic and Mishnaic Hebrew.

"By decree of" (3:7): *mi-taʿam*. *Taʿam* in the sense of "decree" is an Aramaism (cf. *teʿem* in Dan. 3:10 and Ezra 4:21), found in the Hebrew books of the Bible only here.

"Myriad" (4:11): *ribbo*. The pre-exilic books always use the form *revavah* (except for Ps. 68:18). In addition to here, *ribbo* also occurs in Daniel, Ezra, Nehemiah, Chronicles, and Mishnaic Hebrew.

Grammatical and Syntactic Forms

"How can you be sleeping so soundly!" (lit., "What's the matter with you, sleeping [one]"–1:6): *mah lekha nirdam*: In classical Hebrew, the question would be phrased *mah lekha ki nirdamta* (lit., "What's the matter with you that you have fallen asleep") with the preposition *ki* introducing the inflected second-person perfect (cf. Judg. 18:23). This form, with no preposition and the present participle, first appears in Ezek. 18:22 and is typical of Mishnaic Hebrew.

"Lots" (1:7): *goralot*. The older books always use the singular *goral*. The very same procedure is referred to in the plural here, in Nehemiah, Chronicles, the Dead Sea Scrolls, and Mishnaic Hebrew.

"The next day" (4:7): *le-moḥorat*. This form occurs here, in 1 Chron. 29:21, and regularly in Mishnaic Hebrew; elsewhere in the Bible we find the form *mi-moḥorat*.

Idioms

"The God of Heaven" (1:9): *Elohei ha-shamayim*. This epithet is extremely rare in the older books of the Bible (Gen. 24:3, 7; Ps. 136:26), but common in Daniel, Ezra, Nehemiah, Chronicles, and the apocryphal books of Judith and Tobias.

"Great and small alike" (3:5): *mi-gedolam ve-ʿad qetanam*. In the older books, the idiom for the entire population always places the small before the great; the reverse order is found only here, in Esther, and in Chronicles, and is considered to be a "diachronic chiasm" (see Hurvitz).

"This was a great evil to" (i.e., "displeased"–4:1): *va-yeraʿ ʾel*. The older idiom is *va-yeraʿ be-ʿeinei* (lit., "it was evil in the eyes of"). The eyes disappear here, in Nehemiah (2:10 and 13:8), and in Mishnaic Hebrew.

"Compassionate and gracious" (4:2): *ḥannun ve-raḥum*. This, too, is probably a "diachronic chiasm"; in the first presentation of the Thirteen Divine Attributes (Exod. 34:6), the order is "gracious and compassionate." Compassion comes first here and in Joel, Nehemiah, and Chronicles (both forms are used in Psalms).

Orthography

"Innocent" (1:14): *naqiʾ*. Written with a final *ʾalef* only here and in Joel 4:19, in the "full" late spelling common in the Dead Sea Scrolls. (As an isolated phenomenon this cannot be used for dating purposes, however, since *qali*, "parched corn/grain," is written with an appended silent *'alef* in 1 Sam. 17:17 and without it in 2 Sam. 17:28.)

It follows from all these illustrations that the book was composed by an author who lived during the Second Temple period and wrote in classical Biblical language but unwittingly incorporated various elements of his contemporary dialect.

Date of Composition

In the Book of Ben Sira, written in the early second century B.C.E., the "Twelve Prophets" are described as a single unit (49:10). It follows that by his time the Book of Jonah was already part of the Minor Prophets. This sets the latest date when the book could have been written. The unmistakably postexilic elements in its language (see "Language," p. xli) and its clear dependence on the Book of Jeremiah (see "Links between Jonah and Other Biblical Books," p. xxxviii) determine the earliest possible date—the period of the return to Zion. Similarly, the apolitical description of Nineveh as a metropolis whose inhabitants rob one another, and not as the capital of an Assyrian empire that plunders and oppresses subject nations, destroys Samaria, and exiles Israel, requires dating the book after the conquest of Assyria by Babylonia in the year 612 B.C.E. Kaufmann (pp. 279–284) did not believe it plausible that the memory of the wicked Assyrians who destroyed the kingdom of Israel would fade from readers' hearts; accordingly he felt compelled to date the composition of the book to the period *before* the campaigns of Tiglath-Pileser III in the Land of Israel, that is, just about the time when Jonah son of Amittai delivered his prophecies to Jeroboam II. He attempted to dismiss the linguistic evidence with the argument that what sounded like later Hebrew were merely indications of the northern dialect, to which, despite our scanty knowledge thereof, he attributed all the "later" phenomena. But the study of later biblical Hebrew has developed appreciably since Kaufmann wrote. In addition, even scholars such as Landes and Almbladh, who sought to make maximum use of the available information on the northern dialect, were forced to acknowledge that there remains a hard core of later phenomena that require a postexilic date for the composition of the book.

It is possible that the narrator himself is trying to tell readers that Jonah's deliverance of Nineveh need not trouble them, since "Nineveh *was* [formerly] a great city to God" but is no longer so today (see Comment to 3:3). On the other hand, the author seems unaware that the phrase "the king and his nobles" implausibly ascribes to the king of Nineveh a uniquely Persian procedure—the inclusion of the royal council in the issuing of decrees (see Comment to 3:7).

We conclude, then, that the Book of Jonah was written during the Second Temple period but have no way to determine whether it should be dated as early as the late sixth century or the fifth or even fourth century B.C.E. Nor is there any real basis to the various attempts to determine from its theme the book's specific audience, against whose opinions or vacillations it was directed. Since an examination of the language of the frame tale of the Book of Job—with its generic similarity to Jonah (see "Story or History?", p. xvii)—indicates that it too was written during the Second Temple period, we can say that the broad topic of theodicy—justifying God's ways with His creatures—was a matter of deep concern to those generations.

The Text

The Hebrew Text   The scroll of the Minor Prophets found in one of the caves of Wadi Muraba'at and dated to the beginning of the second century C.E. (before the Bar Kokhba rebellion) is the oldest text that has survived. Jonah is preserved almost intact and is practically identical with the consonantal Masoretic text (except for three minor discrepancies, of which the most interesting is *naqi,* without the final *'alef,* in 1:14). We cannot rely on the Aleppo Codex, the most prominent representative of the Ben Asher textual tradition, because of the Minor Prophets only Hosea and Amos (through 8:12) survive. We must rely instead on the Leningrad Codex B19a, written in the year 1009. The vocalized and cantillated text of this manuscript is almost identical to the standard text crystallized in the Venice edition of the rabbinic Bible *(Miqra'ot gedolot)* of 1525–1526. Medieval manuscripts do not offer any significant differences either. Of the seven textual variants recorded by De Rossi, only one is interesting: instead of *ve-qara' 'eleha,* "cry out *to* it" (3:2), one manuscript reads *ve-qara' 'aleha,* "cry out *against* it," as in 1:2 (the Aramaic Targum Jonathan also renders both verses in the same way).

The Greek Text of the Septuagint   The Septuagint antedates the Wadi Muraba'at scroll by about 300 years. Because it is a translation, however, its evidence as to the Hebrew original is only indirect. The text it reflects is almost certainly the Masoretic version, except for the following variants, of which only the first seems to be preferable to the Masoretic text: (1) The clause "because of whom has this evil come upon us" (1:8) is not found in two of the three principal manuscripts of the Septuagint or in two medieval Hebrew manuscripts, lending substance to the conjecture that this is really a marginal gloss that was miscopied into the text. (2) "A servant of the LORD" (1:9) instead of "a Hebrew." (3) "Currents engulfed me" (plural instead of singular–2:4). (4) Future tenses with a jussive force—"let them be covered . . . [let them] cry . . . let every person turn back" (3:8)—were understood as the inverted future with a past signification—"they covered themselves . . . they cried . . . they turned back." As a result, verse 8 is not the continuation of the royal decree but a description of the Ninevites' acts of repentance. This seems to have entailed prefixing the word "saying" to the beginning of verse 9, so that this verse becomes something like the penitents' self-encouragement. (5) "Three days more" (3:4) instead of "forty days more"! (6) "To cast shade" (4:6) instead of "to save."

Conjectural Emendations   The excellent state of preservation of the text almost totally exempts commentators from the need to propose conjectural emendations. The plausibility of the following conjectures is considered in the body of the commentary: (1) deleting the clause "because of whom has this evil come upon us" (1:8) as a marginal note that has crept into the text; (2) deleting the words "for so he had told them" (1:10) as a marginal note; (3) leaving out "into the deep" (2:4) as a doubling of "into the heart of the sea"; (4) reading "how" *('eikh)* instead of "nevertheless" *('akh)* (2:5); (5) deleting "man and beast" (3:8) as a repetition from the previous verse; and (6) moving 4:5 to follow 3:4 because it ostensibly interrupts the chronological order. As we shall see, the first two of these are attempts to solve authentic problems, but the other four will be seen to be unnecessary (see commentary ad loc.).

THE COMMENTARY TO
JONAH

CHAPTER 1

The Command and Its Violation   (vv. 1:1–3)

The Judge of all the earth dispatches a Hebrew prophet to the gentile metropolis to proclaim its imminent destruction. But the man, who has heard the word of the Lord and been commanded to make it known to the city, whose wickedness has risen to Heaven like the outcry of Sodom and Gomorrah, does not heed the divine injunction and instead boards a ship bound for Tarshish, to run away from the Lord. He knows full well that there is no place on sea or land outside the dominion of his God: not only is this dominion embodied in the very act of dispatching him to distant Nineveh, but Jonah bears explicit witness to it when he tells the sailors, "I fear the LORD, the God of Heaven, who made both the sea and the dry land" (1:9). According to the *Mekhilta of Rabbi Ishmael* (Pesaḥ 1; ed. Hurvitz-Rabin, p. 3), Jonah thought he could frustrate his prophetic mission by leaving the land of revelation: "Jonah said: I will go outside the Land of Israel, to a place where the Divine Presence is not revealed. . . . This is like the slave of a *kohen,* who ran away from his master and said, 'I will go to the cemetery, where my master cannot follow me.'" This interpretation was adopted by Saadiah Gaon (*Beliefs and Opinions* 3,5), Rashi, Abraham bar Ḥiyya, Abraham ibn Ezra, Judah ha-Levi (*Kuzari* 2,14), and David Kimḥi. But it seems difficult to ascribe this idea to Jonah, since at the end of the book we are told that the Lord appeared to Jonah in Nineveh and east of it (4:5, 9), without any indication that this refutes his initial hypothesis. It is more likely that Jonah fled westward in an attempt to turn his back on the One who sent him. Indeed, the intimate association that biblical psychology postulates between presence in a place and willingness to act—which finds its quintessential expression in the ambiguity of the word *hinneni,* "here I am" (e.g., "Israel said to Joseph, '. . . Come, I will send you to them.' He answered, 'Here I am'" [Gen. 37:13; see also 22:7 and 27:18])—reveals Jonah's flight to be an act of rebellion. Jonah is not satisfied with passive disobedience to the word of the Lord; instead of starting for Nineveh as instructed, he gets up without a word and does precisely the opposite. It is true that Moses, Gideon, and Jeremiah all recoil initially from their missions; unlike Jonah, however, they express their opposition in words (Exod. 3:11; 4:10, 13; Judg. 6:13, 15; Jer. 1:6), so that it is possible for the Lord to persuade them to bow to its yoke. Superficially, Jonah resembles Elijah, who flees to the wilderness and begs to die (1 Kings 19). But Elijah does this only after he has performed his mission, in response to Jezebel's threat against his life and his sense that he has failed. Only Samson resembles Jonah in his unwillingness to assume the mission itself; his evasion leads him, too, to the antithetical action: instead of saving Israel in its war against the Philistines, he seeks his private happiness in the love of Philistine women. These comparisons reinforce our astonishment at the rebellion by the prophet of the Lord, which is not mitigated by any information about his motives. Instead, the thunderous silence of the hero, which is part of the plot, is amplified by the curious silence of the narrator, which is part of the narrative art (see Introduction, "Why Is the Motive of Jonah's Flight Concealed until Chapter 4?" p. xxv).

   1. The word of the LORD came   The nature of the book is implicit in its opening. The story, which depicts one incident in the life of a prophet, begins directly with the first stage of the plot—the Lord's revelation to His prophet. The formula "the word of the LORD came to . . . saying" is fairly common in prophetic narratives, but except for this case it always comes in the body of the story and not at its beginning (e.g., 1 Sam. 15:10; 2 Sam.

1 The word of the LORD came to Jonah son of Amittai: ² Arise and go to Nineveh, that great city, and

אַ וַיְהִי דְּבַר־יְהֹוָה אֶל־יוֹנָה בֶן־אֲמִתַּי לֵאמֹר:
² קוּם לֵךְ אֶל־נִינְוֵה הָעִיר הַגְּדוֹלָה וּקְרָא

7:4; 1 Kings 13:20; and especially the Elijah stories, whose affinity to our story is evident: 1 Kings 17:2, 8; 21:17, 28; and later in our book, 3:1). In the later prophetic books, however, it also serves as the introduction to a prophetic utterance (dozens of times in Ezekiel, such as 6:1 and 7:1) or a prophetic mission (Ezek. 12:1; 37:15; Zech. 6:9), just as it does here.

Jonah son of Amittai   The prophet is introduced by his full name, a form appropriate to the superscription of a book (e.g., Jer. 1:1; Prov. 1:1) and to the first mention of the protagonist of a story (e.g., Judg. 4:4, 6; 2 Kings 18:1). Because it is most implausible that there were two prophets whose names and whose fathers' names were identical, we may infer that the prophet in this story is the same Jonah son of Amittai from Gath-hepher, active during the reign of Jeroboam son of Joash (787–747 B.C.E.), who is mentioned in 2 Kings 14:25. (On the possible significance of this implicit identification, see Introduction, "The Identification of Jonah with the Prophet Who Brought Good Tidings to Sinful Israel," p. xxxviii.) Striking in any case is the absence of an exposition that would anchor the plot in a given place, time, and circumstances. It seems likely that this omission was intended to apprise readers that they must not adduce biographical or historical factors in an attempt to explain the prophet's otherwise unmotivated flight.

2.   Nineveh, that great city   Nineveh was one of the oldest and largest cities in Mesopotamia and is so described in Gen. 10:11–12 (where we also have the epithet "great city," although it is not clear whether it refers to Nineveh or to Calah). The expression "that great city" is repeated later in the story, once with regard to its territory (3:3) and once with regard to its population (4:11). Here, however, it is part of the definition of the prophet's mission. Nineveh's size is mentioned, not to emphasize the difficulty of the task, but to highlight its importance—as is the size of the city, so is the magnitude of its wickedness (compare this with Lot's entreaty, in Gen. 19:20, that God not destroy the city of Zoar, with the argument that, because it is small, its sins are of no great weight).

and cry out against it   Although Targum Jonathan renders both this verse and 3:2 as "prophesy against it," we ought to distinguish the verb *q-r-ʾ*, "call/cry," followed by the preposition ʿ*al* from the same verb followed by the preposition ʾ*el*. The former denotes the proclamation of impending destruction (e.g., "the man of God, at the command of the LORD, cried out *against* the altar" [1 Kings 13:1]; see also Jer. 25:29 and Ps. 105:16), and even indictment and condemnation (e.g., "He will cry out to the LORD *against* you, and you will incur guilt" [Deut. 15:9]), and can therefore stand alone without an accusative (as this verse is punctuated by the cantillation signs). The denotation of the latter, by contrast, depends upon the context supplied by a direct object: "cry out to it the message" (3:2). The other occurrences of the latter form in Jonah all refer to prayer (1:6, 14; 2:3; 3:8).

for   Sometimes the conjunction *ki* is used to introduce indirect speech (e.g., "Why did you not tell me *that* she was your wife? [Gen. 12:18]; see also Job 36:10). Here, though, the causative sense is preferable, both because "cry out against it" needs no complement and because it seems likely that the first injunction, which Jonah did not fulfill, was thematically identical with the later one, in which the content is stated explicitly: "Forty days more..." (3:4).

their wickedness has come up before Me   The clamor of the accumulated iniquity has reached Heaven and come before the Lord, as in "Let all their wrongdoing come before You" (Lam. 1:22)—take notice of the evil they are doing. The subject, "their wickedness," echoes the language used about the generation of the Flood: "The LORD saw cry out against it; for their wickedness has come up before Me. ³Jonah, however, arose to flee to Tarshish from the presence of the LORD. He went down to

עָלֶיהָ כִּי־עָלְתָה רָעָתָם לְפָנָי: ³ וַיָּקָם יוֹנָה לִבְרֹחַ תַּרְשִׁישָׁה מִלִּפְנֵי יְהוָה וַיֵּרֶד יָפוֹ וַיִּמְצָא

how great was man's wickedness on earth" (Gen. 6:5). The predicate "has come up before me" recapitulates God's words about Sodom: "I will go down to see whether they have acted altogether according to the outcry that has reached Me" (Gen. 18:21). But unlike those two destructions, which were not preceded by a public warning, here Jonah is dispatched to inform the condemned of their imminent doom. Note that the reference is to "Nineveh, that great city," and not to the kingdom of Assyria. "Their wickedness" accordingly refers to the malefactions of its citizens toward one another (cf. 3:8), not to the imperialist crimes for which the prophet Nahum reproves the king of Assyria: "All who hear the news about you clap their hands over you. For who has not suffered from your constant malice?" (Nah. 3:19).

3. *Jonah, however, arose to flee* Jeremiah speaks of his inability to hold in the word of the Lord: "I thought, 'I will not mention Him, no more will I speak in His name'—but [His word] was like a raging fire in my heart, shut up in my bones; I could not hold it in, I was helpless" (Jer. 20:9). It is probably the intensity of the divine injunction that keeps Jonah from ignoring it and continuing his routine. Although he knows that there is no respite from the word of the Lord, he hopes that there may be some escape from it. The rebellion embodied by his diametrically contrary action is expressed by the partial coincidence between the phrasing of the divine injunction, "Arise and go to Nineveh," and that of its anti-fulfillment, "Jonah...arose to flee to Tarshish." Here we have another echo of the Elijah stories (this time inverted). The earlier prophet's utter obedience is expressed by the full linguistic coincidence of "Arise and go to Zarephath" and "he arose and went to Zarephath" (1 Kings 17:9–10). Jonah, by contrast, does indeed arise and set out—but in the opposite direction.

to Tarshish Josephus (*Antiquities of the Jews* 9,10,2) identified Tarshish with "Thrassos in Cilicia" (a port city in southeastern Asia Minor), evidently on the basis of the phonetic resemblance of the biblical and Greek names. It seems more plausible, however, to identify it with the Phoenician colony of Tartessus, which seems to have been located in southern Spain, west of the Straits of Gibraltar, in a region rich in silver and other metals. M. Eilat believes that other biblical references to Tarshish support this identification. The prophecies about "crown-wearing Tyre" contain repeated references to the dependence of its merchants and sailors on "ships of Tarshish" (Isa. 23:1–14; Ezek. 27:25) and accentuate the import of "silver, iron, tin, and lead" from Tarshish (Ezek. 27:12; cf. Jer. 10:9). In three different passages (Isa. 60:6–9; Ezek. 38:13; Ps. 72:10), the full geographical extent of the known world is delimited by Tarshish at one end and Sheba at the other. Given that the latter lies in the east (in the southern Arabian peninsula), at the end of the overland caravan route, the other must lie in the far west, at the end of the maritime trade route. Indeed, this location of Tarshish in the uttermost west (and not north of the Land of Israel, as Josephus would have it) accords with the threefold mention of Tarshish in this verse: first to denote Jonah's destination, second when he finds a ship that is sailing there, and a third time when he boards the vessel. This indicates that Jonah was not merely seeking to leave the Land of Israel by sea and flee to whatever destination the first ship might carry him, but in fact was trying to sail to the farthest possible point from his assigned destination.

to flee...from the presence of the LORD Abraham ibn Ezra distinguishes between flight *mi-penei,* which connotes a distancing motivated by fear, and flight *mi-lifnei,* the form used here, which implies a rupture of contact and turning of one's back, as in "Cain

Joppa and found a ship going to Tarshish. He paid the fare and went down into it to go with the others to Tarshish, away from the presence of the LORD.

אֲנִיָּה | בָּאָה תַרְשִׁישׁ וַיִּתֵּן שְׂכָרָהּ וַיֵּרֶד בָּהּ לָבוֹא עִמָּהֶם תַּרְשִׁישָׁה מִלִּפְנֵי יְהוָה:

left the presence (mi-lifnei) of the LORD" (Gen. 4:16). However, his assertion that this is the only place in the Bible where flight is not followed by mi-penei (i.e., "from") is not quite accurate: for example, "I will send a plague ahead of you, and it shall drive out from before you (mi-le-fanekha) the Hivites, the Canaanites, and the Hittites" (Exod. 23:28); "the Arameans fled from (mi-lifnei) Israel" (1 Chron. 19:18)—although the parallel passage in 2 Sam. 10:18 has the preposition mi-penei. Still, the distinction itself is valid and can be supported by the use of the root b-r-ḥ to denote a rapid departure that is not necessarily associated with flight inspired by terror (e.g., "Back with you at once [beraḥ lekha] to your own place!" [Num. 24:11]; see also Isa. 48:20). Perhaps this too is an intentional contrast with the story of Elijah: whereas the faithful messenger says of himself that he stood before the One who sent him like a slave before his master ("As the LORD lives, the God of Israel before whom I stood" [1 Kings 17:1 and 18:15]; see also 2 Kings 3:14 and 5:16; Jer. 15:19), Jonah seeks to rupture this link.

Going　　The root b-w-ʾ can mean not only "come" but also, as here, "go" (as in "Are your brothers to go to war?..." (Num. 32:6). The form used here (ba'ah) is the present participle, as indicated by the accent on the final syllable (the third-person-singular past tense is accented on the penult; see Rashi on Gen. 29:9).

He paid the [lit. "its"] fare　　The feminine possessive attached to the word "fare" supports the homily of R. Johanan, "He paid the fare of the entire ship" (B. Nedarim 38a); in other words, he sought to expedite the ship's departure by ensuring that it would not have to wait for additional passengers. More plausible thematically, however, is Abraham ibn Ezra's demurral: "Not its entire fare, but only what he had to pay for his own share." Modern commentators continue to disagree on this point, but it is in any case clear that the mention of this unimportant detail is intended to emphasize that to realize his escape Jonah was willing not only to leave his home but even to pay for his journey. This fare must have been quite high, given the duration of a coasting journey from one end of the Mediterranean to the other. According to the Mishnah (Baba Batra 3,2), in Roman times the journey to Spain could take a full year, evidently because of the need to restock provisions frequently at ports along the way, wait for favorable winds, and trade the cargo.

and went down into it　　This is the second descent in this verse: first he "went down" to Joppa, on the coast, and now he goes down into the ship (cf. Isa. 42:10 ["You who sail (lit. 'go down to') the sea"] and Ps. 107:23 ["Others go down to the sea in ships"], as well as the English idiom in Masefield's "I will go down to the sea again"). Later there is a third descent, into the hold of the vessel (v. 5). Each of these descents makes perfect sense thematically, but not all are absolutely necessary for the story. We may accordingly see them as intentional repetition meant to accentuate the prophet's _vertical_ flight from his God, who dwells on high. Later, when he is hurled into the sea, the extent of this vertical flight increases, as a direct consequence of the failure of his _horizontal_ flight westward. (On desperate flight in all directions, including downward, compare: "If they burrow down to Sheol,... if they ascend to heaven,... if they hide on the top of Carmel,... if they conceal themselves from My sight at the bottom of the sea" [Amos 9:2–3]; "If I ascend to heaven,... if I descend to Sheol,... if I take wing with the dawn to come to rest on the western horizon" [Ps. 139:8–9].)

to go with the others　　Since it is self-evident that Jonah is traveling with the ship's crew (and any other passengers who may be aboard), the superfluous "with the others"

[4] But the LORD cast a great wind upon the sea, and such a great storm came upon the sea that the ship

וַיהוָה הֵטִיל רֽוּחַ־גְּדוֹלָה אֶל־הַיָּם וַֽיְהִי סַֽעַר־ גָּדוֹל בַּיָּם וְהָאֳנִיָּה חִשְּׁבָה לְהִשָּׁבֵֽר: [5] וַיִּֽירְאוּ

must be meant to express another dimension of his flight from his prophetic function—the desire to escape the existential isolation of one who carries the word of the Lord and to find acceptance as just one more member of society.

　　　away from the presence of the LORD　　This definition of the objective of Jonah's flight was already presented at the start of the verse. Evidently the narrator repeats it at the end of the verse in order to highlight the magnitude of Jonah's audacity and spur readers to wonder: Will the Lord frustrate Jonah's flight? Or will He ignore it and allow the prophet to slough off the task to which he is so vigorously opposed? Will the anguished protest be accepted and the mission itself cancelled? (On the structure of verse 3, see the Introduction, p. xxix).

In the Storm-Tossed Ship:
The Sailors' Fear of the Lord versus Jonah's Rebellion　　(vv. 1:4–16)

The opening words of this scene make readers aware of what the characters will have to discover in its course: that it is the Lord who is pursuing His servant by means of the great storm. The reactions of the gentile sailors and the prophet of the Lord to the looming peril of death by drowning are poles apart and quite the opposite of what one might have expected. In contrast to the sailors' clear vision and perfect compliance with the voice of the Lord, as it rises from the waves of the storm-tossed sea, Jonah shuts his eyes against the truth and, when compelled to open them, persists in his stubborn refusal to obey. On the surface, there is nothing more absurd than a prophet of the Lord who seals his mouth against prayer at a time when the sailors of diverse nations and creeds are crying out with all their heart "each to his own god" (v. 5). However, Jonah's willingness to die, rather than ask his God to save him, indicates that (pace the prevalent opinion among scholars) the scene is not satirical but pathetic. The bald contrast is not meant to ridicule the prophet but to add a dramatic depth to his determined silence toward God and stoic indifference to death and thereby make tangible the magnitude of his crisis of faith. The captain's question, "How can you be sleeping so soundly?" (v. 6) fully manifests the disparity between the sailors and their passenger: they are terrified of death and make supernal efforts—both spiritual and mechanical—to escape it; but he remains tranquil, calm, and passive, not excessively frightened by death, because it can help him escape from something far worse. The sailors' energetic inquiry into the cause of the tempest, which relies on a lottery that singles out precisely the one traveler who did not pray to his God, compels him to give up his stolid indifference and recognize that it is indeed the Lord who is pursuing him. In this way Jonah realizes that not only has his plan "to go with the others to Tarshish" (v. 3) been frustrated; if he continues his path of inaction, they will drown with him and because of him. To prevent this, he accepts full responsibility for the storm and does not hesitate to tell them that they can avoid being caught up in his punishment by casting him overboard. His ethical response toward them is matched by theirs toward him. They row frantically, in a desperate attempt to escape the tragedy of rescuing themselves at the price of his life. The failure of this noble enterprise leaves Jonah only one way out—to was in danger of breaking up. ⁵ The sailors were afraid and cried out, each to his own god; and they cast the ship's cargo into the sea to make it lighter for them.

הַמַּלָּחִים וַיִּזְעֲקוּ אִישׁ אֶל־אֱלֹהָיו וַיָּטִלוּ אֶת־הַכֵּלִים אֲשֶׁר בָּאֳנִיָּה אֶל־הַיָּם לְהָקֵל מֵעֲלֵיהֶם

abandon his rebellion. But he holds fast to his refusal to address the Lord in prayer and continues his flight unto death. As the ship scene draws to its end, we are told nothing more about his fate (a temporary gap); readers assume (erroneously) that Jonah drowns and conclude (correctly) that, because of him, the crew attained to fear of the Lord and worshipped him with a sacrifice and vows. Jonah courageously detached them from his quarrel with his God and accurately foretold that the sea would stop raging as soon as they cast him into it. As a result, at the end of the scene our thoughts return to Jonah, even though he is no longer on stage, and we are astonished to discover that the prophet cannot escape prophecy. His prophetic function adheres to Jonah wherever he goes; he magnified the name of the Lord among the gentiles even when he ran away from Him. (On the concentric structure of this scene, see the Introduction, pp. xxix–xxx.)

4. But the LORD cast The word order in Hebrew, with the subject at the beginning of the sentence, necessarily followed by the perfect form of the verb, serves to emphasize the doer of the action (as in "Now the serpent was the shrewdest" [Gen. 3:1]). Whereas everything went smoothly in the first stage of his flight and Jonah's five actions followed one after another without hindrance (v. 3), the deferred counteraction now erupts in full force, with the narrator emphasizing that its source is the Lord.

cast a ... wind This is the only occurrence in Scripture of the expression "cast a wind." Evidently the narrator employed a nonstandard idiom in order to unify the entire sequence of events by means of a key word: the casting of the wind onto the sea whipped up the storm; the casting of the cargo into the sea was in vain (v. 5). Jonah understood that only his being cast into the sea could calm it, because then the divine pursuit would attain its objective (v. 12), and that is precisely what came to pass (v. 15).

was in danger Literally "thought intently" or "intended to": that is, was about to break up. The metaphoric language attributes consciousness to the ship in the common sense of intention and planning (cf. "you intended me harm" [Gen. 50:20]; 1 Sam. 18:25). Accordingly, Targum Jonathan rendered it as "wanted *or* sought to break up," on the semantic model of "he was on the verge of tears [lit. 'sought to cry']" (Gen. 43:30). Similarly, in Mishnaic Hebrew we find the phrase "if he sought to slumber" (M. Yoma 1,7) in the sense of "was about to fall asleep."

of breaking up Even in the open sea a ship can break up as the result of a strong wind (see Ezek. 27:26 and Ps. 48:8). As in all the other verses that describe divine intervention in the course of events, this intervention is highlighted by an alliterative play on words: *hishevah le-hishaver* (see Introduction, "Wordplay," p. xxxiv).

5. The sailors The Hebrew word *mallah,* "sailor," is borrowed from Sumerian, by way of the Akkadian *malāhu.* Later they are referred to simply as "the men" (vv. 10, 13, 16). Evidently the designation of their profession (cf. Ezek. 27:9, 27, 29) is meant not only to clarify their identity but also to illuminate the magnitude of the peril by means of the terror and helplessness of skilled seamen (cf. Ps. 107:27–28).

each to his own god The diverse origins of merchant-vessel crews are also attested to by Ezekiel (27:8–9).

cargo This is how we should understand the Hebrew word *kelim,* which generally means "tools," "implements," or "vessels"; see, for example, Exod. 22:6, where it means "portable property." When their prayers are not answered, the sailors endeavor to save

But Jonah, meanwhile, went down into the hold of the vessel where he lay down and fell asleep. ⁶The

וְיוֹנָה יָרַד אֶל־יַרְכְּתֵי הַסְּפִינָה וַיִּשְׁכַּב וַיֵּרָדַם:
⁶ וַיִּקְרַב אֵלָיו רַב הַחֹבֵל וַיֹּאמֶר לוֹ מַה־לְּךָ

their lives by giving up their property (lightening its burden raises a ship's waterline, a procedure believed to be helpful in this situation).

But Jonah, meanwhile, went down The word order in Hebrew, subject before a verb in the *pa‛al* (perfect), expresses either the pluperfect—an action that preceded another one that has just been related (as in "Meanwhile *Laban had gone* to shear his sheep" [Gen. 31:19]—i.e., before Jacob and his family decamped from Haran)—or an action simultaneous with and contrasted to the one that has just been recounted (as in "Cain brought an offering . . . and *Abel . . . brought . . .*" [Gen. 4:3–4]; and "he embraced his brother Benjamin around the neck . . . and *Benjamin wept* on his neck" [Gen. 45:14]). Because Jonah's action is contrasted with that of the sailors, it seems likely that he went down into the hold and fell asleep at the very same time as the sailors were struggling, through prayer and action, to save the ship. Jonah's willful refusal to consider the possible religious significance of the tempest is another expression of his flight from the Lord; his ability to sleep at such an hour is the first manifestation of his inclination to prefer death over life. In this yearning to escape from the prophetic function into the bosom of death, via sleep, he again resembles Elijah (1 Kings 19:4–5).

hold The Hebrew *yarketei* is the construct form of *yarkatayim* (as in "And for the *rear* of the Tabernacle . . . for the corners of the Tabernacle at the *rear*" [Exod. 26:22–23]), which is itself the dual of *yerekhah* (as in "his *flank* shall rest on Sidon" [Gen. 49:13]). The basic meaning of the term is "the farthest end" (cf. "Now David and his men were sitting in the *back* of the cave" [1 Sam. 24:4]).

the vessel The Hebrew *sefinah* (borrowed from the Akkadian *sapīnatu,* by way of Aramaic), occurs only here in Scripture but is found in Mishnaic Hebrew. Until now (vv. 4 and 5) the narrator has spoken of a "ship" (Heb. *’oniyyah*); here he uses instead a word derived from the root *s-p-n,* whose fundamental meaning is "cover" (as in "It was *paneled* above with cedar" [1 Kings 7:3]), to indicate that the ship had a full deck and a covered hold.

6. **The captain** Hebrew *rav ha-ḥovel,* literally "the chief of the linesmen"; sailors are called "linesmen" (cf. "And all the oarsmen and mariners, all the *linesmen* of the sea" [Ezek. 27:29]) because their job is to tend the lines attached to the mast and sail. Unique to this verse, however, is the use of the singular *ḥovel* as a collective noun designating the entire crew (cf. "a thousand *craftsman* and *smith*" [2 Kings 24:16]). Unique, too, in Scripture is the use of *rav,* "master," plus a singular noun to indicate the chief of a body of men; the construction is borrowed from Akkadian (cf. the Assyrian title "the Rabshakeh" [2 Kings 18:17], as well as the Hebraicized forms "Rab-saris" and "Rab-mag" [Jer. 39:13]) or from Aramaic (Onkelos renders *sar ha-tabbaḥim* [Gen. 39:1]—frequently Englished as "chief steward"—as *rav qatulya,* "chief of killers," i.e., chief of staff).

How can you In rhetorical questions, the Hebrew idiom *mah lekha* expresses vigorous reproof (cf.: "What, then, *is the good* of your going to Egypt? . . ." [Jer. 2:18]; "*How dare you* crush My people? . . ." [Isa. 3:15]; "to the wicked, God said: '*Who are you* to recite My laws? . . .'" [Ps. 50:16]).

Arise and cry to your god He who refuses to rebuke Nineveh is himself rebuked. But the prophet who refuses to cry against Nineveh at the Lord's behest cannot cry to Him in prayer (as Elijah does on behalf of the widow's son, 1 Kings 17:20–21). It is quite natural,

נֵרָדָּם קוּם קְרָא אֶל־אֱלֹהֶיךָ אוּלַי יִתְעַשֵּׁת
הָאֱלֹהִים לָנוּ וְלֹא נֹאבֵד: 7 וַיֹּאמְרוּ אִישׁ אֶל־
רֵעֵהוּ לְכוּ וְנַפִּילָה גוֹרָלוֹת וְנֵדְעָה בְּשֶׁלְּמִי

captain approached him and said to him, "How can you be sleeping so soundly! Arise and cry to your god! Perhaps the god will give us a thought and we will not perish." ⁷ The men said to one another, "Let

then, that Jonah does not comply with the captain's request and even closes his ears against this echo of the divine injunction that is clearly sounded from "*Arise* and go to Nineveh . . . *and cry* against it" (v. 2).

Perhaps The captain expresses the cautious hope that a deity who has not yet been approached may help, while evincing comprehension of the nature of true prayer, which never presumes to impose itself magically on God (cf. "You have been guilty of a great sin. Yet I will now go up to the LORD; *perhaps* I may win forgiveness for your sin" [Exod. 32:30]; as well as Amos 5:15 and Lam. 3:29; see also B. Hagigah 4b).

will give us a thought Compare "May the LORD give a thought to me. You are my help and my rescuer" (Ps. 40:18). The Hebrew verb *yitʿashet* occurs only here, but its meaning can be inferred from the related nouns *ʿeshtonot* ("on that day his *plans* come to nothing" [Ps. 146:4]) and *ʿashtot* ("In the *thought* of the complacent" [Job 12:5]) and from the cognate Aramaic verb *ʿashit* ("the king *considered* setting him over the whole kingdom" [Dan. 6:4]).

and we will not perish So *that* we will not perish (the Hebrew *vav* of result).

7. The men said to one another The narrator does not tell us how Jonah dodged the captain's urgent request—by stubborn silence or an evasive explanation. This lacuna protracts Jonah's silence as far as the narrative is concerned. Readers are left to conclude from the sailors' consultations that Jonah neither prayed to his God nor told them why he could not do so.

lots Here in the plural, but in the singular ("the lot fell") at the end of the verse. The change seems to be not a stylistic variation but a distinction between the process, which is phrased in the plural (see Introduction, "Grammatical and Syntactic Forms," p. xlii), and its result, phrased in the singular (the same distinction is found in 1 Chron. 26:14). We may assume that successive rounds of lots were cast, in a procedure similar to the multistage process used to discover the identity of the guilty party who had sequestered some of the proscribed property after the conquest of Jericho (Josh. 7:14–18) and of the person who had violated Saul's oath before the battle of Michmas (1 Sam. 14:40–42). Lots were also used to help resolve disputes: "The lot puts an end to strife and separates those locked in dispute" (Prov. 18:18). No one challenged the validity of the method, because it was viewed as divinely guided: "Lots are cast into the lap; the decision depends on the LORD" (Prov. 16:33). The pebbles were generally thrown into a concealed spot, like the folds of one's cloak or a vessel, and then withdrawn (Num. 33:54) or lifted out (Lev. 16:9).

that we may know In order *that* we may know (the Hebrew *vav* of purpose). Unlike the prophet, who wishes to shut his eyes, the sailors want to know. They understand that all of their efforts have failed because they do not know the reason for the storm. Now they conduct a systematic inquiry based on the ethico-religious assumption that the ship is laboring under a burden of sin and only the discovery and purging of the guilt can prevent its destruction (cf. Josh. 7:11–13 and 1 Sam. 14:37–39).

They cast lots There are three references to casting lots in the verse: once each for the planning, the execution, and the outcome. The slackening of the narrative pace involves readers in the tension felt by the characters themselves: what will the lottery indicate?

הָרָעָה הַזֹּאת לָנוּ וַיַּפִּלוּ גּוֹרָלוֹת וַיִּפֹּל הַגּוֹרָל
עַל־יוֹנָה: ⁸ וַיֹּאמְרוּ אֵלָיו הַגִּידָה־נָּא לָנוּ
בַּאֲשֶׁר לְמִי־הָרָעָה הַזֹּאת לָנוּ מַה־מְּלַאכְתְּךָ
וּמֵאַיִן תָּבוֹא מָה אַרְצֶךָ וְאֵי־מִזֶּה עַם אָתָּה:
⁹ וַיֹּאמֶר אֲלֵיהֶם עִבְרִי אָנֹכִי וְאֶת־יְהוָֹה אֱלֹהֵי

us cast lots that we may know on whose account this evil has come upon us." They cast lots and the lot fell on Jonah. ⁸ They said to him, "Tell us, because of whom has this evil come upon us? What is your business? Where have you come from? What is your country, and of what people are you?" ⁹ "I am a

on whose account Literally "on account of [the guilt] that is whose?" The unique Hebrew compound *be-shellemi* agglomerates the causal *bet* (as in "*on account of* this man's life" [v. 14]), the relative pronoun *she-* (which often replaces *'asher* in the later books of the Bible), the genitive *le-* (as in "at the door of Elisha's house" [2 Kings 5:9]), and the interrogative *mi*, "who."

8. ***because of whom has this evil come upon us*** This clause is phrased identically to the question in verse 7, except that the particle *she-* has been supplanted by the relative pronoun *'asher*. Because the outcome of the lottery has already fully answered the question, it is implausible that the sailors repeated it to Jonah. For this reason, David Kimḥi was forced to explain the clause, not as a question, but as an indictment—"you are the one on whose account this distress has come upon us!" This is also the preference of Ehrlich, who suggests that here *mi* is not an interrogative but a nominative pronoun (as in "*he who* has sinned against Me" [Exod. 32:33]), so that *le-mi* is equivalent to a possessive: "Tell us, (you) on *whose* account this evil has come upon us, what is your business?" Many, however, doubt the reliability of the Masoretic text, noting that these words are not found in two of the three major ancient manuscripts of the Septuagint (Vatican and Sinai) and from two medieval Hebrew manuscripts (de Rossi, vol. 3, p. 194). They conjecture that the clause is a marginal note originally written adjacent to the previous verse to gloss the strange word *be-shellemi*. But one cannot be sure that the agreement between the Septuagint and Hebrew manuscripts constitutes decisive proof of an ancient and authentic text, since it is possible that the omission is the result of an independent lapse by both the Greek and Hebrew copyists, whose eyes accidentally jumped from the first to the second *lanu*.

What is your business? The sailors do not rashly act against the passenger who first made himself suspicious by refusing to pray and has now been incriminated by the lottery. In order for their response to appease the deity who has sent the storm, they must know who Jonah's God is and how he transgressed against Him. They shower him with basic questions about his identity, some of them overlapping (for multiple voices in collective speech, see Judg. 18:3, 9–10; 1 Sam. 9:12–13), aimed at learning about his occupation, origins, and ethnic affiliation.

9. ***I am a Hebrew*** Jonah begins with their last question (Sasson, p. 115), ignores the question "What is your business?" (perhaps because he was uneasy about describing himself as a prophet of the Lord), and provides a fuller-than-expected answer to the last two questions (in the manner of the Gibeonites to Joshua [Josh. 9:9] and Hezekiah to Isaiah [2 Kings 20:14]). The designation "Hebrew" is appropriate to his situation; it is used chiefly in contact with members of other nations (as in Gen. 14:13 and 41:12; Exod. 1:16 and 3:18; and 1 Sam. 4:6). The Septuagint reading, "a servant of the LORD" instead of "a Hebrew," was evidently caused by the similarity in shape of the letters *resh* and *dalet*, plus understanding the letter *yud* as an abbreviation for the Divine Name (thus *'eVeDY* instead of *'iVRY*). (There is evidence that the Hebrew text used by the Septuagint translators sometimes resorted to this shorthand form: "my house" for the Masoretic "House of the LORD" in Judg. 19:18; "my wrath" for "wrath of the LORD" in Jer. 6:11.) The translators may have also been influenced by the reference to Jonah as "the servant" of the LORD God

Hebrew," he replied. "I fear the LORD, the God of Heaven, who made both the sea and the dry land." ¹⁰ The men feared greatly, and they said to him,

הַשָּׁמַ֔יִם אֲנִ֣י יָרֵ֑א אֲשֶׁר־עָשָׂ֥ה אֶת־הַיָּ֖ם וְאֶת־הַיַּבָּשָֽׁה׃ ^י וַיִּֽירְא֤וּ הָֽאֲנָשִׁים֙ יִרְאָ֣ה גְדוֹלָ֔ה

of Israel in 2 Kings 14:25. The Greek text is implausible for two reasons, however: not only does it leave the question about Jonah's national affiliation unanswered, it seems rather far-fetched that a runaway servant would identify himself with reference to his master.

I fear the LORD, the God of Heaven   More literally, "[It is] the LORD, the God of Heaven, [that] I fear." Had Jonah sought to obscure his responsibility for the tempest, he would have provided no more than bare factual responses concerning his national and religious affiliation and would not have focused attention on the attributes of his God by the unusual word order, which puts the object before the subject and verb. The elaboration he appends to the name of his God is meant to eliminate all doubt concerning that deity's absolute dominion over the entire universe. The epithet "the God of heaven" is found almost exclusively in books written during the Persian period (outside of Daniel, Ezra, Nehemiah, and 2 Chronicles, it appears only in Gen. 24:3 and 7 and in Ps. 136:26). Like "a Hebrew," it is used mainly in contexts of interaction with gentiles, whether addressed to (e.g., Ezra 5:11 and Neh. 2:20) or spoken by them (e.g., 2 Chron. 36:23 and Ezra 6:9–10).

I fear   This is not an empty declaration that Jonah worships the Lord ("fear" or "awe" in the conventional meaning of fealty and obedience, as in "your servant *revered* the LORD" [2 Kings 4:1]). It is rather implicit acknowledgment of his personal responsibility for their predicament because he falls under the direct jurisdiction of the Lord (cf. "your children might prevent our children from *worshipping* the LORD" [Josh. 22:25], which refers to religious affiliation only) and the punitive action—the storm—is clearly directed against him. The difference between *'anokhi* in the first clause and *'ani* in the second is merely a matter of stylistic variation; both mean simply "I" (Ben David, p. 61).

who made both the sea and the dry land   The Creator is the master of His creation (cf. Isa. 45:9); accordingly the Lord who created the three components of the universe (see Exod. 20:11: "in six days the LORD made heaven and earth and sea, and all that is in them") reigns over all without let or hindrance (cf. "Whatever the LORD desires He does, in heaven and earth, in the seas and all the depths" [Ps. 135:6]). Here the author preferred the less-common *yabashah*, "dry land," to *'erez*, "land," because it expresses the contrast with liquid water more starkly (see the narratives of the splitting of the Red Sea [Exod. 14:16] and of the Jordan [Josh. 4:22]) and also because it is a key word all through the story (1:13 and 2:11) (Sasson).

10.   The men feared greatly   Literally "the men feared a great fear": The intensification of their emotion expressed by the internal accusative helps convey the fact that their initial fear of the storm (v. 5) was magnified when they learned that they were in the power of a mighty Deity from whom there is no escape (cf. "If a man enters a hiding place, do I not see him?—says the LORD. For I fill both heaven and earth—declares the LORD" [Jer. 23:24]; also Amos 9:2–4). The juxtaposition of the gentiles' "great fear" to Jonah's "I fear" is not meant to cast the fugitive prophet's fear of heaven in a ridiculous light (as many hold), but to define by contrast their respective positions at this moment: he recognizes the sovereignty of the Lord but is not afraid to disobey Him; whereas they fear His mighty hand but do not recognize His sovereignty.

What have you done!   Literally "What [is] this [that] you have done?!" Once again strong reproof overtakes the prophet who himself refuses to utter a reproof. The deictic *zot*, "this," gives greater force to the interrogative *mah*, "what"; the phrase *mah zot* is frequent in rebukes (e.g., Gen. 12:18 and 29:25; Judg. 2:2). The fact that the sailors say

"What have you done!" for the men knew that he was fleeing from the presence of the LORD—for so he had told them. ¹¹ Then they said to him, "What shall we do to you to make the sea calm around us?" For the sea was growing more and more stormy. ¹² He answered, "Lift me and cast me into the sea, and the sea will calm down for you; for I know that this

וַיֹּאמְרוּ אֵלָיו מַה־זֹּאת עָשִׂיתָ כִּי־יָדְעוּ
הָאֲנָשִׁים כִּי־מִלִּפְנֵי יְהוָה הוּא בֹרֵחַ כִּי הִגִּיד
לָהֶם: ¹¹ וַיֹּאמְרוּ אֵלָיו מַה־נַּעֲשֶׂה לָּךְ וְיִשְׁתֹּק
הַיָּם מֵעָלֵינוּ כִּי הַיָּם הוֹלֵךְ וְסֹעֵר: ¹² וַיֹּאמֶר
אֲלֵיהֶם שָׂאוּנִי וַהֲטִילֻנִי אֶל־הַיָּם וְיִשְׁתֹּק הַיָּם
מֵעֲלֵיכֶם כִּי יוֹדֵעַ אָנִי כִּי בְשֶׁלִּי הַסַּעַר הַגָּדוֹל

merely "have you done"—and not "have you done *to us*" (which is the usual practice of rebukers: e.g., Gen. 26:10; Exod. 14:11; Judg. 15:11)—adds another admirable trait to their collective image: they are not protesting the catastrophe he has brought upon them, but expressing their shock at the very act of running away from a God who cannot be escaped!

for the men knew   This explanatory note makes plain that their question is a rhetorical exclamation rather than a request for information. They do not expect an answer, because their desire to know (v. 7) what action "caused" the storm has already been satisfied. The prolixity of the second half of the verse (an unusual string of three subordinate clauses, each introduced by the particle *ki*—"*for* the men knew *that* he was fleeing... *for* so he had told them") and the divergence from chronological order (the men's fear placed ahead of its cause) are unexpected. Some conjecture that "he had told them" is a marginal gloss that has found its way into the main text. This explanation assumes that Jonah had already made the sailors aware that he was fleeing from the Lord; since, however, this sequence is not certain—Jonah could be pursued on account of any transgression against God or man—the note was added to make plain that he had told them more than is reported to us. If, on the other hand, the clause is indeed authentic, it is difficult to explain why the narrator adopted such indirection instead of adding "and I am running away from Him" to Jonah's first speech to the sailors. With regard to the structure of this scene (see table 1 in the Introduction, p. xxx), the flashback satisfies the needs of the concentric pattern by opposing the "discovery of the culprit" (F), which leads to "questions to determine the nature of his crime" (G), with a "reproving question" (G') that is explained by the flashback: "the crime is already known to them" (F') in the second part (flashbacks of this sort can also be found in Est. 3:4 and Neh. 8:9). It may also be that the narrator prefers to focus on the sailors' consciousness rather than report Jonah's actual speech, so that their understanding of the gravity of the situation—"for the men knew"—can precede Jonah's own (incomplete) comprehension—"for I know" (see Comment to v. 12).

11.   *What shall we do to you*   With the storm raging ever more fiercely, the sailors realize that they must do something to Jonah that will rescue them from the consequences of his action (v. 10), that is, from the death by drowning that is about to engulf both him and them at the hands of his God who is pursuing him. The fact that they consult with him indicates that they recoil from any rash or hasty action. Jonah, for his part, can see their question as a last chance to give up his flight.

12.   *Lift me and cast me into the sea*   Jonah submits to his Pursuer but persists in his rebellion. He chooses death—passive suicide (cf. Judg. 9:54 and 16:30; 1 Sam. 31:4)—to abandoning his flight and prophesying against Nineveh. Being cast into the depths of the sea will be the fourth and evidently final descent in the course of his vertical flight.

for I know   Whereas the sailors' knowledge refers to his sin—"that he was fleeing from the presence of the LORD" (v. 10)—his knowledge relates to its consequences for them—"that this great storm came upon you on my account." Thus Jonah sidesteps the question of guilt while accepting full responsibility for their safety and converting his

great storm came upon you on my account."
¹³ Nevertheless, the men rowed hard to regain the
dry land, but they could not, for the sea was growing
more and more stormy about them. ¹⁴ Then they cried
out to the LORD: "Oh, please, LORD, do not let us
perish on account of this man's life. Do not hold us
guilty of killing an innocent person! For You, O
LORD, by Your will, have brought this about." ¹⁵ And

הַזֶּה עֲלֵיכֶם: ¹³ וַיַּחְתְּרוּ הָאֲנָשִׁים לְהָשִׁיב אֶל־
הַיַּבָּשָׁה וְלֹא יָכֹלוּ כִּי הַיָּם הוֹלֵךְ וְסֹעֵר
עֲלֵיהֶם: ¹⁴ וַיִּקְרְאוּ אֶל־יְהֹוָה וַיֹּאמְרוּ אָנָּה יְהֹוָה
אַל־נָא נֹאבְדָה בְּנֶפֶשׁ הָאִישׁ הַזֶּה וְאַל־תִּתֵּן
עָלֵינוּ דָּם נָקִיא כִּי־אַתָּה יְהֹוָה כַּאֲשֶׁר חָפַצְתָּ
עָשִׂיתָ: ¹⁵ וַיִּשְׂאוּ אֶת־יוֹנָה וַיְטִלֻהוּ אֶל־הַיָּם

imminent drowning from an act of punishment into a deed that will save them. The
Mishnah pronounces sentence on a prophet who refuses to utter his message: "He that
suppresses his prophecy,... his death is at the hands of Heaven, as it is written, 'I myself
will call him to account' (Deut. 18:19)" (M. Sanhedrin 11,5); the Gemara applies this to
Jonah (B. Sanhedrin 89a). Abraham bar Ḥiyya, however, associated the Lord's pursuit of
Jonah with Ezek. 33:8: "When I say to the wicked, 'Wicked man, you shall die,' but you
have not spoken to warn the wicked man against his way, he, that wicked man, shall die for
his sins, but I will demand a reckoning for his blood from you."

on my account   On account of my action. (On the form of the Hebrew compound
be-shelli, see Comment to v. 7.)

13.   *the men rowed hard*   The other occurrences of the root *ḥ-t-r* in the Bible
refer to digging in the ground ("If they *burrow down* to Sheol" [Amos 9:2]) or piercing
through walls ("If the thief is seized while *tunneling*" [Exod. 22:1]; "so I *broke through* the
wall" [Ezek. 8:8]). Here it is perhaps being used metaphorically for the splitting of the
water by the action of the oars. The sailors ignore Jonah's appalling advice (although its
logic is undeniable) and redouble their attempts to escape by applying the techniques of
their craft. But these are foredoomed to failure, since "the dry land" is no less under the
dominion of Jonah's God than is the sea (v. 9 [Sasson]). Their utter failure and the
augmented force of the storm compel them to return to their earlier conclusion that their
identification with the fugitive makes them accomplices in his flight and subject to his
punishment. Seeing that their pangs of conscience about throwing Jonah overboard are
appreciated to their merit, they realize that there is no escaping the duty imposed on them
to execute the divine sentence.

14.   *Then they called out to the LORD*   The contrast between the idolatrous sailors
and the prophet of the Lord reaches its zenith: not only do they call upon the Lord his
God when he himself refuses to pray, but in utter contrast to his stubborn rejection of his
mission, they accept the burden of being the instruments of God's will. They pray that,
since they are bowing to His purpose ("For You, O LORD, by Your will, have brought this
about") and subordinating their fear of sin to the performance of His mission ("Do not
hold us guilty of killing an innocent person"), their taking the life of this man not be
accounted as a criminal deed ("do not let us perish on account of this man's life").

innocent   In Joel 4:19, too, the adjective *naqi'* is spelled with a terminal *'alef* to
emphasize the *i* sound. This is also the typical orthography of the Dead Sea Scrolls,
for example, "the blood of the innocent" (Isa. 59:7) in the Isaiah scroll 1QIsaᵃ
(see Introduction, p. xlii).

15.   *they lifted Jonah and cast him into the sea*   Echoing Jonah's instruction to
them, "Lift me and cast me" (v. 12). For the purpose of the plot, however, "they cast him
into the sea" would have sufficed. The Midrash expands the superfluous words into an
entire scene that portrays the sailors' reluctance to shed innocent blood by understanding

they lifted Jonah and cast him into the sea, and the sea stopped raging. ¹⁶ The men feared the Lord greatly; they offered a sacrifice to the Lord and they made vows.

וַיִּקְחוּ אֶת־יוֹנָה וַיְטִלֻהוּ אֶל־הַיָּם וַיַּעֲמֹד הַיָּם מִזַּעְפּוֹ: ¹⁶ וַיִּירְאוּ הָאֲנָשִׁים יִרְאָה גְדוֹלָה אֶת־יְהוָה וַיִּזְבְּחוּ־זֶבַח לַיהוָה וַיִּדְּרוּ נְדָרִים:

"lifting" as meaning "out of the sea": "R. Shimon said: . . . They cast him in as far as his ankles and the sea stopped raging. They lifted him back to them and the sea was wracked by storm. They cast him in as far as his navel and the sea stopped raging. They lifted him back to them and the sea was wracked by storm. They cast him in as far as his neck [and the sea stopped raging. Again they lifted him back to them and the sea was wracked by storm against them. They cast him in all the way and at once the sea stopped raging]" (*Yalkut Shimoni* 2,550, completed from *Pirkei de-Rabbi Eliezer* 10).

and cast him   For the verb *t-w-l* as a key word in the narrative, see Comment to verse 4.

16.   The men feared   As soon as the sailors complied with the dreadful will of Jonah's God and executed their mission under compulsion, the sea stopped raging, exactly as Jonah had predicted. Just as the towering waves had filled their hearts with "a great fear" (v. 10), now the uncanny calm on the sea opened their hearts to "a great fear of the Lord."

a sacrifice . . . vows   Their sacrifice is to be understood not as a collective but as a genuine singular: to express their spontaneous thanks they sacrifice to the Lord, right there on the deck of the ship, one of the animals they had taken aboard for food. Their vows, however, are in the plural: to express their continuing gratitude and perhaps also to make it widely known, each of them vows to bring a sacrifice when he reaches his destination. Kaufmann (p. 282) notes that this does not mean that they abandoned their pagan creeds and adopted the faith of Israel; it is simply a magnification of the glory of the Lord among the nations, such as we find in the stories of Elijah (1 Kings 17:24) and Elisha (2 Kings 5:15–18; 6:12, 23; 8:7–15).

CHAPTER 2

In the Belly of the Fish: Submission   (vv. 2:1–11)

Just as the great storm blocked Jonah's course to Tarshish, the great fish closes off the gates of death. For three days and three nights the prophet is trapped and imprisoned, resolutely silent in the belly of the fish just as he remained mute in the hold of the ship. At first he could delude himself that the fish had been sent not only to save him from drowning but also to return him to dry land, and hope that his preferring death to performing his mission had moved the Lord to relieve him of that task. But as the days and nights pass, the prophet realizes his true situation: both doors—to death and to life—can be opened only by prayer. He is led to renew contact with the Lord not by the threatening waves, but by the closed belly of the fish; his mouth is not opened by the fear of death, but by the powerlessness of an in-between state that is neither life nor death.

We should ask, though, why his prayer resembles a hymn of thanksgiving for deliverance rather than a psalm of entreaty, as we might expect. An even greater difficulty is that the psalm concludes with a ceremonial promise to fulfill his vow and offer thanksgiving sacrifices in the Temple, while totally omitting the main point—an entreaty to be forgiven for his flight and a promise to repent and undertake his mission to Nineveh.

Whatever value the various forced explanations and dubious answers proposed to these difficulties may have, it is outweighed by their drawbacks, since all of them undercut the exegetical criteria on which the *peshat* method of interpretation is based. What is more, any reconciliation of the story and the psalm obscures the unique meaning of each (see Introduction, "The Unity of the Book and the Provenance of the Psalm," p. xxxv).

The tension between the psalm and the circumstances in which it is uttered is largely dissipated if we assume that there is no literary reason for ascribing its composition to Jonah or even to the author of the book. The prayer from the belly of the fish may have been understood as the borrowing of a preexisting psalm, which, like the standard liturgy we say all the time, is only approximately suited to the situation of the worshipper and necessarily applies to his current needs only with some freeness. Of course, there is a major exegetical difference between viewing the psalm as an integral part of the story and as a later accretion. If the author himself was responsible for the incorporation of the psalm into the story, the commentator must find its main message in what it does *not* say. That is, Jonah is portrayed as having selected, from the available store of prayers, a psalm of thanksgiving and vows rather than one of regret and repentance, with the intention that his involuntary supplication say no more than he is capable of. Forced to submit to the greater might of the Deity, he is still very far from recognizing His justice and therefore states only the praises of God who holds the keys of life and death and who answers those who call upon Him in their distress.

On the other hand, if the psalm was interpolated into the story by someone who was less sensitive than the author to the character of the prophet, and his struggles with God through the various stages of the plot, commentators should give greater weight to the many motifs in the psalm that may be understood as redressing Jonah's improper silence on the ship. This rectification helps diminish the perplexing disparity between the exemplary conduct of the gentile sailors and the behavior of the fugitive prophet. I tend to this second view and believe that the person responsible for the interpolation selected this psalm from among all the hymns of thanksgiving he knew: first, because of its repeated references to drowning in the depths of the sea; second, because of the many statements that, taken out of the poetical context and interpreted flexibly (chiefly by making past tenses refer to the future), depict Jonah, though still unwilling to fulfill his duty as a prophet, as no whit inferior to the idolators of the crew. The sailors called on the Lord in their distress (1:14), and so does Jonah now (albeit in the past tense; cf. Ps. 120:1): "Out of my distress I called" (2:3), with an emphasis on the contrast between his mute slumber in the hold of the ship and the present prayer: "From the belly of Sheol I cried out" (2:3). The Lord responded to the sailors' prayer and saved them ("and the sea stopped raging" [1:15]); Jonah too is confident that his prayer from the belly of the fish will be answered (again in the past tense): "From the belly of Sheol I cried out, and You heard my voice" (2:3). They were wise enough to treat the tempest as a theological problem ("on whose account this evil has come upon us" [1:7]); he too refers to his sinking through the billows as a heaven-sent punishment: "The current engulfed me; all Your breakers and billows swept over me" (2:4). They saw his flight as a grievous sin ("What have you done!" [1:10]); he goes so far as to present the sin of running away as the punishment of being cut off—"I have been driven away out of Your sight" (2:5). They saw their casting of Jonah into the sea as fulfilling the will of God ("For You, O LORD, by Your will, have brought this about" [1:14]); in precisely the same fashion he attributes it to the Lord: "You cast me into the deep, into the heart of the sea" (2:4). They arrived at fear of heaven as a result of their miraculous delivery ("The men feared the LORD greatly" [1:16]); he sincerely acknowledges his rescue from drowning: "Yet You brought my life up from the pit, O LORD my God" (2:7). They expressed their gratitude in sacrifice and vows (1:16); he too accepts the duty of publicizing the miracle in this fashion: "But I, with loud thanksgiving, will sacrifice to You; what I have vowed I will perform" (2:10). Finally, he may even highlight his superiority to them by means of an anti-pagan polemic: "They who cling to empty folly will give up their bounty. But I..." (2:9–10).

Clearing the author of responsibility for the prayer enables us to gloss it from two different perspectives: (1) Taking the prayer in its narrative context, we must accept its negative message or break it down into separate statements whose unity is imposed externally by their application to the sailors' actions in chapter 1 (as explained above). (2) Viewing it as freestanding—a psalm like those in the Book of Psalms—we can analyze it as a well-constructed hymn with a sophisticated structure, a clear generic affiliation (a psalm of thanksgiving), and a clear theme—the glory of prayer that rises from Sheol to the sanctuary and brings redemption to one who is lost (as explained below). Because the psalms frequently evoke drowning as an image of calamity from which there is no escape (e.g., "Rescue me from the mire; let me not sink; let me be rescued from my enemies, and from the watery depths" [Ps. 69:15]; see also Ps. 71:20), here too the detailed description of drowning may be only an expanded metaphor in which drowning symbolizes the utter helplessness from which only the Lord can provide salvation.

The five-stanza psalm has an almost uniform meter (2 + 3), except in the middle stanza, and can be summarized as follows:

1. The call from the depths is answered by the One who hears prayers (v. 3).
2. Drowning in the sea as banishment from intimacy with the Lord and rescue as a return to His sanctuary (vv. 4–5).
3. Drowning in the sea as being caught in Sheol and rescue as a return to the land of the living (vv. 6–7).
4. The prayer of the almost-extinguished soul reaches the divine sanctuary (v. 8).
5. The fealty of the person delivered to his rescuer: a thanksgiving prayer and thanksgiving sacrifices (vv. 9–10).

We can understand the structure of the psalm only if we recognize that it does not have an internal chronological sequence (distress—prayer—response—thanksgiving). The opening stanza contains two of the classic hallmarks of thanksgiving psalms. The first of these—beginning the psalm with its essential point (with the consequent anticipation of the later situation)—is a personal testimony of a prayer from the depths of adversity that was heard and answered (cf. Pss. 30:2–4; 116:1–2). The second is the combined address—to the Lord (in the second person) and about Him (in the third person) in the ears of the congregation of His righteous ones (cf. Pss. 30:2–6; 66:13–17).

As a result of this deviation from chronological sequence, the concrete description of drowning is postponed until the second and third stanzas, which share several properties: greater length than stanzas one and four, consistent use of the second person in addressing the Lord, and the same internal structure. In the first two lines of the second stanza and in the (augmented) first line of the third stanza, the speaker relates how he was swept away and surrounded by the formidable waters and was plunged into the depths of the sea. The next line in each of these stanzas reconstructs the terrible despair that passed through his mind while he was sinking into the billows; their closing lines express the magnificence of the climactic deliverance. The parallelism of the two stanzas is emphasized by the appearance in the first line of each of *yesoveveni,* "engulfed me"; they are further melded into a single unit by the contrast between "You cast me," which opens the second stanza, and "You brought up," which concludes the third: the God who cast him down into the depths of the sea is the same God who raises him up and redeems him from death. Against the background of this similarity of theme and structure, the vast difference in perspective is unmistakable. In the second stanza, drowning is described in religious terms: the affliction comes directly from the Lord, the finality of death is expressed by a total separation from God, and the essence of deliverance is the renewal of communion with

2 The Lord appointed a great fish to swallow Jonah; and Jonah was in the belly of the fish three days and three nights. ²Then Jonah prayed to the Lord his

ב וַיְמַן יְהוָה דָּג גָּדוֹל לִבְלֹעַ אֶת־יוֹנָה וַיְהִי יוֹנָה בִּמְעֵי הַדָּג שְׁלֹשָׁה יָמִים וּשְׁלֹשָׁה לֵילוֹת:

Him. In the third stanza, however, the terrors of drowning are described in existential terms, with no religious dimension, but with more substance and immediacy—death as a descent from which there is no ascent, rescue as regaining life itself.

The fourth stanza returns to the first with regard to its length (only two lines), the mixing of the second and third persons in reference to the Lord, and especially its theme—the miracle of being answered from afar when on the threshold of death. The fifth stanza, though, stands alone, as indicated both by its theme and future tenses. The man who was saved, who yearned for the Holy Temple (v. 5) and was answered from it (v. 8), now comes to the Sanctuary to repay his rescuer by declaring the nonentity of idols, by proclaiming his gratitude (in the second person), by fulfilling his vows, and by exalting his savior (in the third person) before the assembled congregation (cf. Pss. 66:13–17; 107:31; 116:12–19). The prayer of the drowning man who cries out for help (*qoli,* "my voice" [v. 3]) at the beginning of the psalm turns into the thanksgiving hymn of one who has been saved (*qol todah,* "loud thanksgiving" [v. 10]) at its end.

In sum, everything we have said about the formal sophistication and thematic unity of the psalm indicates that (according to the common critical view) the widespread use of psalmodic idioms (see the body of the commentary) does not detract from its literary unity and poetic distinctiveness.

1. *appointed* The root *m-n-h* in the *pi'el* (intensive) signifies a command and commission when it refers to human beings ("the guard whom the chief officer *had put in charge* of Daniel" [Dan. 1:11]; "Some of them *were in charge* of the vessels" [1 Chron. 9:29]). It denotes preparation and allocation when it refers to food ("the king, who *allotted* food and drink to you" [Dan. 1:10]) or destiny ("Nights of misery have been *apportioned* to me" [Job 7:3]). The first sense is more appropriate here, given the personification of the fish in verse 11 ("The Lord commanded the fish"). In fact, in both places (as well as in the other occurrences of this verb [4:6, 7, 8]) the Septuagint renders it as an injunction, a sense found explicitly in a similar context in Amos 9:3 ("There I will command the serpent to bite them") (see Comment to v. 11).

The Lord appointed The Hebrew uses a conversive future (imperfect) followed by the subject (*va-yeman YHWH),* indicating a simple past, rather than the subject followed by a perfect verb (*ve-YHWH minah),* which would have the sense of the English past perfect. That is, the narrator did not want to emphasize that the Lord's intervention came right after the prophet was cast into the sea. On the other hand, it seems unreasonable to understand the simple past as indicating that Jonah was rescued only after the sailors had offered their sacrifice, in other words, that Jonah had a lengthy struggle in the water before he was swallowed by the fish. More plausible is the conclusion that the narrator preferred this form because it leaves the incident in the narrative present and renders it more dramatic, while relegating whatever intervened between Jonah's being swallowed by the waves and being swallowed by the fish outside the purview of the story.

a great fish Like "a great city" (1:2), "a great wind" (1:4), and "a great fear" (1:10), the fish that will swallow Jonah is noteworthy for its size.

to swallow The verb *b-l-'* does not necessarily have a negative connotation (e.g., "like an early fig before the fruit harvest—whoever sees it *swallows* it while it is still in his hand" [Isa. 28:4]). Its basic denotation is "to bring down into the inside"; hence it is used for being consumed alive (e.g., "the earth opened its mouth and *swallowed* them up. . . .

God from the belly of the fish. ³ He said: Out of my distress I called to the Lord,

וַיִּתְפַּלֵּל יוֹנָה אֶל־יְהוָה אֱלֹהָיו מִמְּעֵי הַדָּגָה׃
וַיֹּאמֶר קָרָאתִי מִצָּרָה לִי

They went down alive into Sheol" [Num. 16:32–33]; see also Ps. 124:3 and 6 and Prov. 1:12), and this is its meaning here as well.

three days This is a common idiom to denote a period that is long, but not too long; for example, "We arrived in Jerusalem and stayed there three days" (Ezra 8:32; see also Neh. 2:11). But there are some activities, such as fasting, for which three days *is* a long time: "he had eaten no food and drunk no water for three days and three nights" (1 Sam. 30:12; see also Esther 4:16). The addition of "and three nights" highlights the slow passage of time in Jonah's consciousness (cf. Exod. 24:18 and 1 Kings 19:8; and see Introduction, p. xxxvii, first paragraph).

2. the Lord his God The designation of the Lord as Jonah's God links this verse with the captain's speech (1:6) and with Jonah's own self-description as one who fears the Lord (1:9). This echo is probably intended to tell us that, when he prays, Jonah has at long last submitted to the authority of his God (cf. Deut. 17:19). This expression also appears in the body of the psalm (v. 7), but there it expresses the intimacy of gratitude.

from the belly David Kimḥi notes that the proclitic prepositional *mi-* in "*from* the belly" is not an indication of physical location, a mere variation on a prefixed *bet* ("in"), in which case "from the belly" would be equivalent to "in the belly." It is rather a deliberate choice to indicate that he prayed *as a result* (another meaning of the prefix *mem*) of his distress; so too in v. 3, "From the belly of Sheol I cried out." This observation is verified also by the first words of the psalm itself: "Out of my distress *(mi-ẓarah li)* I called to the Lord" (v. 3).

the fish The feminine form *dagah* is normally a collective noun (as in "the *fish* in the Nile will die" [Exod. 7:18]). It is difficult to explain why it is used here. Perhaps it is simply a case of elegant variation, with *dagah* used as in Mishnaic Hebrew (this was suggested by Ben David [p. 61]). In the Midrash, however, *dagah* is understood as denoting a female fish and used to illustrate the obstinacy of Jonah, who refused to pray until forced to do so, not only by the pressure of time, but also by the constraints of space: "Jonah was in the belly of the [masculine] fish for three days and did not pray. The Holy One, Blessed be He, said: 'I made him a spacious place in the belly of the fish so that he would not be in pain, but he still will not pray to me! I shall prepare for him a pregnant fish carrying 365,000 fry, so that he will be in pain and pray to me'" (*Midrash Jonah,* p. 98).

3. Out of my distress The opening of Psalm 120 uses a similar trope and construction (a dative instead of a possessive): "In my distress I called to the Lord" (Ps. 120:1). Another reference to prayer uttered out of affliction is "we shall cry out to You in our distress" (2 Chron. 20:9).

And He answered me The Lord's immediate response to those who call on him is a frequent topic in Psalms; see, for example, Pss. 20:10; 34:5; and 138:3.

From the belly of Sheol "Lowermost Sheol" (Ps. 86:13) is the lowest circle of the universe, to which all the dead descend (including the righteous: "I will go down mourning to my son in Sheol" [Gen. 37:35]) and where they dwell as "shades" (see Isa. 14:9 and 26:14). Here Sheol is personified as having a belly; elsewhere in the Bible we find that its mouth gapes to swallow the lawless (Isa. 5:14) and that it is never sated (Prov. 27:20). The supplicant feels that he has already been swallowed up in the innermost recesses of Sheol (cf. "I am at the brink of Sheol. I am numbered with those who go down to the Pit" [Ps. 88:4–5]); accordingly he views his deliverance not as averting death but as actual

And He answered me;
From the belly of Sheol I cried out,
And You heard my voice.
4 You cast me into the deep,
Into the heart of the sea,
The current engulfed me;
All Your breakers and billows
Swept over me.

אֶל־יְהוָה וַיַּעֲנֵנִי
מִבֶּטֶן שְׁאוֹל שִׁוַּעְתִּי
שָׁמַעְתָּ קוֹלִי:
4 וַתַּשְׁלִיכֵנִי מְצוּלָה
בִּלְבַב יַמִּים
וְנָהָר יְסֹבְבֵנִי
כָּל־מִשְׁבָּרֶיךָ וְגַלֶּיךָ
עָלַי עָבָרוּ:

resurrection (cf. "O LORD, You brought me up from Sheol, revived me from among those who went down into the Pit" [Ps. 30:4, reading with the *ketib*]). The glory of prayer is that it has the power to save the supplicant from a situation that would have been irreparable without divine intervention (cf. "whoever goes down to Sheol does not come up" [Job 7:9]; 2 Sam. 12:23). The great tension generated by the unexpected sequence of Sheol, crying, and being heard is reinforced by the alliteration: *mi-beten she'ol shivva'ti shama'ta qoli*.

4. You cast me Here, as in Isa. 14:19 ("you were *cast out* of your grave like loathsome carrion"), the verb *hashlekh* has two meanings at the same time: the literal sense of being cast into the water and the figurative senses of being loathsome and rejected—"Do not *cast me out* of Your presence" (Ps. 51:13; see also Ps. 71:9); abandoned—"she *left* the child under one of the bushes" (Gen. 21:15; see also Ezek. 16:5); and unworthy of preservation—"A time for *throwing* stones and a time for gathering stones" (Eccles. 3:5). Because Jonah ascribes this *rejection* (in both the current English sense and the original Latin signification) to the Lord, he also assigns the waves that beset him to God, as if they were his minions—"*Your* breakers and billows."

into the deep The poetic singular is also found in Ps. 69:3: "I am sinking into the slimy deep....I have come into the watery depths." The Hebrew has no explicit preposition to convey the locative "into" (unlike the construction in Neh. 9:11: "You threw their pursuers *into* the depths"). Because of this anomaly and because there are six beats in the line, instead of the five found in almost every other line of the psalm, it has been conjectured that "deep" is a marginal note, originally a gloss on "the heart of the sea," that has been interpolated into the text. Neither argument is decisive, however. First, biblical Hebrew often omits the locative preposition or suffix (e.g., "ships to go [to] Tarshish" [2 Chron. 20:36]; also Gen. 24:27 and 26:23). Second, the meter of biblical poetry is far from the regularity and fixity characteristic of classical Greek and Latin poetry or of Arabic poetry (as will become clear from vv. 6 and 7). Hence we should probably assume that the two indications of place are complementary: "deep" refers to vertical distance underwater, while "the heart of the sea" indicates the horizontal distance from dry land, as in "the way of a ship in heart of the seas" (Prov. 30:19; see also Ezek. 27:25–27).

The current Marine currents, too, are sometimes referred to as *nahar*, "river/stream" (cf. "[I,] who said to the deep, 'Be dry; I will dry up your *currents*'" [Isa. 44:27]; see also Hab. 3:8; Pss. 24:2 and 89:26). In Ugaritic, too, the sea deities who contend against Baal are named both "Lord of the Sea" and "Judge/ruler of the *Stream*."

engulfed me The helpless feeling of someone who sinks in deep water is augmented by the dread of one who is surrounded by a hostile force (cf. Pss. 18:5–6; 118:10–12).

5 וַאֲנִי אָמַרְתִּי

נִגְרַשְׁתִּי מִנֶּגֶד עֵינֶיךָ

אַךְ אוֹסִיף לְהַבִּיט

אֶל־הֵיכַל קָדְשֶׁךָ:

6 אֲפָפוּנִי מַיִם עַד־נֶפֶשׁ

5 I said, I have been driven away
Out of Your sight:
Nevertheless I shall gaze again
Upon Your holy Temple.
6 The waters closed in over me,

All your breakers and billows swept over me Waves that *break* in both the transitive and intransitive senses. The drowning man, swamped by the powerful waves (note the parallelism in 2 Sam. 22:5—"For the breakers of Death encompassed me, the torrents of Belial terrified me"; cf. Ps. 93:4), feels that they are all directed against him: the Hebrew *'alai 'avaru* ("swept over me") alliterates. This phrase recurs word for word in Ps. 42:8.

5. I said, I have been driven away The thoughts of the drowning man, expressed in direct speech, embody the magnitude of his despair (cf. "waters flowed over my head; I said: I am lost!" [Lam. 3:54]: there Hebrew *nigzarti*, here the near-cognate *nigrashti*, a rare passive form that seems to be used only here in this sense). Because he considers that he has been rejected and consigned to drowning by his God, he understands his imminent death as a final dismissal from the Lord's presence and providence (on the latter, cf. Ps. 11:4). In a similar passage (Ps. 31:23), an almost identical statement of despair serves as the contrasting backdrop to unexpected salvation: "Alarmed, I had thought, 'I am thrust out (Hebrew *nigrazti*) of Your sight'; *yet* You listened to my plea for mercy when I cried out to You"; that also seems to be the case here: "Nevertheless I shall gaze again." Those commentators who try to find chronological order in this psalm (ignoring its structure and the parallel between the last parts of vv. 5 and 7) must understand the last clause not as a description of the peripeteia but as an expression of hope, or read *'eikh*, "how" instead of *'akh*, "nevertheless"—along with Theodotion's Greek version.

gaze In the first part of the verse the rupture with the Lord is described as banishment from His field of vision. So, too, in the second part the renewal of the bond is described in terms of sight: pilgrimage as gazing at the Holy Temple (cf. "to gaze upon the beauty of the LORD, to frequent His temple" [Ps. 27:4]).

6. closed in over me This second description of the terrors of drowning begins with the parallel verbs "closed in" and "engulfed"—cf. "Ropes of Death *closed around* me; . . . ropes of Sheol *surrounded* me" (Ps. 18:5–6) (which echoes v. 4 by repeating the word *yesoveveni*, "engulfed me")—applied to the synonymous nouns "waters" and "deep" (see Gen. 1:2; Ezek. 31:4; Pss. 77:17 and 104:6).

over me Literally "as far as the soul": As in Ugaritic and Akkadian, in biblical Hebrew *nefesh* also has the sense of mouth and throat (e.g., "Sheol has opened wide its *gullet* and parted its jaws in a measureless gape" [Isa. 5:14]; see also Eccles. 6:7) and of neck (e.g., "His feet they hurt with fetters; his soul was laid in iron" [Ps. 105:18]; see also Prov. 3:22). The medieval commentators, who did not know that this passage (and the similar phrase in Ps. 69:2) could be understood as a physical description of water reaching the organ of swallowing and breathing, had to assume that the language here is elliptical and must be filled in (e.g., Abraham ibn Ezra's "until my soul was about to die").

Weeds twined Although *suf* usually denotes a plant that grows on the riverbank (e.g., "she . . . placed it among the *reeds* by the bank of the Nile" [Exod. 2:3]; see also Isa. 19:6), here the reference must be to seaweed that wraps itself around the head of the drowning victim.

The deep engulfed me.
Weeds twined around my head.
7 I sank to the base of the mountains,
The bars of the earth behind me forever.
Yet You brought my life up from the pit,
O Lord my God!

תְּהוֹם יְסֹבְבֵנִי
סוּף חָבוּשׁ לְרֹאשִׁי׃
7 לְקִצְבֵי הָרִים יָרַדְתִּי
הָאָרֶץ בְּרִחֶיהָ בַעֲדִי לְעוֹלָם
וַתַּעַל מִשַּׁחַת חַיַּי
יְהוָה אֱלֹהָי׃

7. I sank One frequent use of the root *y-r-d,* "go down, descend," is in reference to death ("they who *descend* into the Pit" [Isa. 38:18]; "those who *go down* into silence" [Ps. 115:17]; "*leading down* to Death's inner chambers" [Prov. 7:27]). Another is in descriptions of drowning ("They *went down* into the depths like a stone" [Exod. 15:5]). It seems likely that both senses are meant here: the speaker is sinking to his death in the depths of the sea. There may also be a contrast to the pilgrimage ascent referred to in vv. 5, 8, and 10: instead of ascending to the top of the mountains, I have sunk to their bases in the depths of the sea.

to the base of the mountains The noun *qezev* (here rendered "base") denotes a form or shape (as in the only other occurrences of the noun in the Bible: "The two cherubim had the same measurements and *proportions*" [1 Kings 6:25; also 7:37]). This seems to be derived from the notion that shapes are cut out; the verb *q-z-v* can have the meaning "cut" (e.g., "he *cut off* a stick" [2 Kings 6:6]). Hence it is possible for *qizvei* to have the same signification as *qazvei,* "boundaries" (e.g., "all the boundaries of the land" [Isa. 26:15]), which is derived from the root *q-z-h/q-z-z,* whose primary meaning is "cut." The Vulgate accordingly renders this phrase as "to the edges of the mountains." The reference seems to be to the foundations of the mountains, which in biblical cosmography reach all the way to the bottom of the sea: "though mountains topple into the sea" (Ps. 46:3). In Ben Sira 16:23, we find "the base *(qizvei)* of the mountains and the foundations of the earth," evidently echoing the present verse and influenced by Deut. 32:22 ("the base of the hills"). Targum Jonathan's rendering is "the roots of the mountains," probably under the influence of Job 28:9.

The bars of the earth behind me forever In the Bible we do not find the image of a gate with reference to the land of the living, but only with reference to the land of the dead: "the gates of Sheol" (Isa. 38:10); "the gates of death" (Pss. 9:14 and 107:18; Job 38:17). Hence it seems likely that here "the earth" *('erez)* is not the dry land that is closing its gates against his return to it, but "the lowest part of the netherworld" *('erez taḥtiyyot)* (Ezek. 32:18) or "the land of the shades" *('erez refa'im)* (Isa. 26:19) that is locking its exit doors behind him. When he descended to the base of the mountains in the heart of the sea, the land of the dead closed its gates behind him forever—"whoever goes down to Sheol does not come up" (Job 7:9; and cf. 10:21–22). Following Ibn Ezra, many assume that the phrase is elliptical and the reader is supposed to supply the missing verb "closed."

Yet You brought my life up from the pit The Hebrew *shaḥat* means simply "pit" (e.g., "He who digs a pit will fall in it" [Prov. 26:27]) or, figuratively, the tomb (e.g., "They shall bring you down to the Pit and you shall die" [Ezek. 28:8]). Deliverance from drowning is described metaphorically as the raising of life itself from the grave ("a metaphor for his soul, which is in truth his vital force," writes Abraham ibn Ezra), as in "He redeems your life from the Pit" (Ps. 103:4).

O Lord my God The vocative intensifies the second-person address: *You* hurled me into the deep and *You* raise up my life from the pit, O Lord my God.

⁸When my life was ebbing away,
I called the Lord to mind;
And my prayer came before You,
Into Your holy Temple.
⁹They who cling to empty folly
Will give up their bounty,

⁸ בְּהִתְעַטֵּף עָלַי נַפְשִׁי

אֶת־יְהוָה זָכָרְתִּי

וַתָּבוֹא אֵלֶיךָ תְּפִלָּתִי

אֶל־הֵיכַל קָדְשֶׁךָ׃

⁹ מְשַׁמְּרִים הַבְלֵי־שָׁוְא

חַסְדָּם יַעֲזֹבוּ׃

8. *ebbing away* Generally philologists distinguish separate roots ʻ-*t*-*f*, said to have no etymological or semantic connection: one meaning "cover" ("the valleys [are] *mantled* with grain" [Ps. 65:14]), the other denoting "physically weakness" ("thus the *feeble ones* went to Laban" [Gen. 30:42]) or "emotional exhaustion" ("Hungry and thirsty, their spirit *failed*. In their adversity they cried to the Lord" [Ps. 107:5–6]; also Pss. 61:3 and 102:1–2), sometimes to the point of fainting ("your infants, who *faint* for hunger at every street corner" [Lam. 2:19]; and perhaps also Ps. 142:4). Yet the fact that the root ʻ-*l*-*f* also has both significations ("she . . . covered her face with a veil and *wrapped* herself up" [Gen. 38:14], on the one hand, and "the sun beat down on Jonah's head, and he *fainted*" [Jon. 4:8], on the other hand), as does the cognate Arabic verb ʻ-*š*-*y*, which means both "to cover" and "to faint," indicates that the two senses of ʻ-*t*-*f* actually appertain to a single polysemous root (L. Kopf, *VT* 9 [1959], pp. 269–270).

I called the Lord to mind Some commentators hold that here the verb *z*-*k*-*r* in the *qal* has the sense of the causative *hifʻil* and means "utter" or "pronounce" His name (as in "but do not *mention* the 'burden of the Lord' any more" [Jer. 23:36]; cf. also Ps. 105:5). If so, the first half of the verse already refers to the prayer mentioned in the second half. It seems more plausible, however, that the sense is indeed "remembering," as supported by the extremely close parallel in Ps. 143:4–6: "My spirit failed within me; my mind was numbed with horror. Then I *thought* of the days of old; I rehearsed all Your deeds, recounted the work of Your hands. I stretched out my hands to You, longing for You like thirsty earth. Selah." Here, like there, we probably have three stages rather than two: at the nadir of emotional and spiritual exhaustion, a glimmering recollection of God fuels a prayer for the Lord's assistance. According to this reading, the actual act of prayer is not mentioned in the verse, but we learn of it indirectly from the suppliant's thanks for the acceptance of his petition in the second half of the verse.

And my prayer came before You What is expressed in Ps. 88:3 as a request—"let my prayer reach You"—is phrased here as a past certainty.

Into Your holy Temple The prayer reached the Lord's dwelling-place from a great distance (cf. "in His temple He heard my voice; my cry to Him reached His ears" [Ps. 18:7]; "May He send you help from the sanctuary, and sustain you from Zion" [Ps. 20:3]), that is, it reaches the earthly sanctuary, which the rescued person yearns to visit (v. 5).

9. They who cling to empty folly Other gods whose divinity is spurious and who are merely vain folly (cf. "They vexed Me with their *futilities*" [Deut. 32:21]; and also "Why then did they anger Me with their images, With alien *futilities*?" [Jer. 8:19]). Relying on the context, both the Septuagint and Targum Jonathan rendered the participle *meshammerim* here in the sense of "worshippers." Given the normal usage of the root *sh*-*m*-*r* in the Bible, however, the idea of "clinging or adhering to" seems better. The parallel passage in Ps. 31:7–8 is of great help in understanding this difficult verse: "I detest those who rely (*ha-shomerim*) on empty folly, but I trust in the Lord. Let me exult and rejoice in Your goodness (*be-ḥasdekha*) when You notice my affliction." It seems unlikely

¹⁰ But I, with loud thanksgiving,
Will sacrifice to You;
What I have vowed I will perform.
Deliverance is the LORD's!
¹¹ The LORD commanded the fish, and it spewed
Jonah out upon dry land.

י וַאֲנִי בְּקוֹל תּוֹדָה
אֶזְבְּחָה־לָּךְ
אֲשֶׁר נָדַרְתִּי אֲשַׁלֵּמָה
יְשׁוּעָתָה לַיהוָה: ס
יא וַיֹּאמֶר יְהוָה לַדָּג וַיָּקֵא אֶת־יוֹנָה אֶל־
הַיַּבָּשָׁה: פ

that the scorn for idolators in both passages is intended to express the Psalmist's superiority to them (as Jonathan translated and Rashi glossed); more plausible is that it is meant to glorify the Lord, who alone merits praise and gratitude. In the parallel passage in Psalms, *ḥesed* should be understood as having its normal sense of a bounty or boon; hence it seems likely that here it denotes the bounty of the "empty folly." If so, the sense of the verse is that those who cling to false gods will abandon their expectation of receiving their bounty (cf. "for my eyes are on Your *favor*" [Ps. 26:3]). Another possibility, also somewhat strained, is that the possessive "their" refers to those who cling to empty folly: eventually they will come to realize that by doing so they are neglecting their own welfare. By contrast, those who adhere to the true God merit to give thanks to Him in the present. In this way, the act of thanksgiving itself (recounted in the next verse) constitutes one of the praises of God, whose devotees will not be disappointed (cf. Ps. 22:5–6).

10. *But I* The adversive Hebrew *vav*.

with loud thanksgiving Thanksgiving is voiced "with joyous shouts" (Pss. 42:5 and 118:15) and is addressed toward both heaven and the celebrating throng: "raising my voice in thanksgiving, and telling all Your wonders" (Ps. 26:7). Giving publicity to the miracle and honoring Him who wrought it are incumbent upon a person who asked for help: "Call upon Me in time of trouble; I will rescue you, and you shall honor Me" (Ps. 50:15; cf. Pss. 30:2, 5, and 13; 116:12–13). Full expression of gratitude has two parts—recounting the story of one's deliverance and offering a sacrifice: "Let them offer thanksgiving sacrifices, and tell His deeds in joyful song" (Ps. 107:22).

I... will sacrifice... I will perform The cohortative form of the verb (a lengthened first-person singular future that expresses intention or desire) and especially the reference to the performance of vows indicate that here the reference is not to the remote future, when the person who has been delivered arrives at the Temple, but to the immediate future—in other words, the present, when he proclaims that by offering the thanksgiving sacrifice he is fulfilling what his lips uttered in his affliction (cf. Pss. 66:13–14 and 116:17–18).

Deliverance The Hebrew *yeshuʿatah* is a poetic form of the normal *yeshuʿah*. It is found twice in Psalms (3:3 and 80:3) and has parallels in other poetic forms, namely, *ʾeimatah* (Exod. 15:16), *sufatah* (Hos. 8:7), *ʿavlatah* (Ezek. 28:15), *ʿezratah* (Ps. 63:8), *ʿefatah* (Job 10:22), and *zaratah* (Ps. 120:1). The clause "Deliverance is the LORD's" stands by itself and ends the psalm with an extraordinarily concise summation of its content—"To the LORD [belongs] deliverance" (Ps. 3:9).

11. *The LORD commanded the fish* The Lord who commanded the fish to swallow Jonah now commands it to spew him forth. This involvement of an animal as a divine emissary to influence the prophet's action is another instance in which Jonah resembles Elijah: "I have commanded the ravens to feed you there" (1 Kings 17:4).

it spewed Just as there is no derogatory connotation to being swallowed (see Comment to v. 1), neither is there one to being spewed out—especially since it comes as the Lord's response to Jonah's prayer. (The verb *palat,* used by Targum Jonathan here, does not have this meaning in biblical Hebrew, and the root *q-y-ʾ* is not found in Aramaic; hence one cannot say that the translator was trying to soften the language of the verse.) The spewing forth at the end of the scene is a return by inversion to the swallowing up at its beginning. Both are at the command of the Lord; but whereas in the first instance we learn of the action only indirectly, subsumed in an infinitive of purpose ("The LORD appointed a great fish to swallow Jonah"), here the actual spewing forth is reported: the Lord commands, and the fish spews Jonah out.

upon dry land In accordance with a divine command Jonah reaches dry land, to which the sailors could not return him (Sasson). Here the story returns to its point of origin. Because this closure of the plot cycle provides no answer to the problem of the unfulfilled injunction with which the story begins, it is really an open ending that requires a sequel (see Tribble, pp. 116–117).

CHAPTER 3

The Repeated Command and Its Fulfillment   (vv. 3:1–3a)

In his prayer, Jonah expressed no readiness to go to Nineveh; nor, when he reaches dry land, does he set off on his mission until he is again commanded to do so. The close parallel between this scene and the opening scene of the story (1:1–3) indicates that this is a new beginning: the plot has returned to its starting point, but on a higher level. The two opening scenes divide the story into two halves of almost equal length, which have parallel contents after the opening scenes as well (see the introductions to the subsequent units). Juxtaposing the two introductions highlights their structural and stylistic parallelism:

Chapter 1

1. *The word of the* LORD *came to Jonah* son of Amittai:

2. *"Arise and go to Nineveh, that great city, and cry out* against it; for their wickedness has come up before Me."

3. *Jonah,* however, *arose* to flee to Tarshish *from the presence of the* LORD. He went down to Joppa and found a ship going to Tarshish. He paid the fare and went down into it to go with the others to Tarshish, away *from the presence of the* LORD.

Chapter 3

1. The *word of the* LORD *came to Jonah* a second time:

2. *"Arise and go to Nineveh, that great city, and cry out* to it the message that I tell you."

3a. *Jonah arose* and went to Nineveh in accordance with *the word of the* LORD.

Both scenes begin with "The word of the LORD came." But whereas the first scene concludes with "from the presence of the LORD *(mi-lifnei YHWH)*" (1:3), sounding a contrasting echo of sorts to "for their wickedness has come up before Me *(mi-le-fanai)*" (1:2), the second scene ends, as it began, with "the word of the LORD" (3:3a), which exactly repeats the language of the beginning, "The word of the LORD." In utter contrast to the first scene, this time the prophet obeys the injunction to go to Nineveh and the narrator

3 The word of the Lord came to Jonah a second time: ² "Arise and go to Nineveh, that great city, and

ג וַיְהִי דְבַר־יְהֹוָה אֶל־יוֹנָה שֵׁנִית לֵאמֹר:
² קוּם לֵךְ אֶל־נִינְוֵה הָעִיר הַגְּדוֹלָה וּקְרָא

emphasizes that he follows his orders to the letter. At the same time, there is a hint to readers that the external compliance is accompanied by internal opposition. The word-for-word repetition of the original command highlights the need for its reiteration, and the stark difference in the phrases that accompany the two versions of the command indicates that if the insubordinate prophet has been subdued, he has not been persuaded. Instead of the rationale given in the first scene—"for their wickedness has come up before Me" (1:2)—here the emphasis is on the duty to obey the command because it is the word of God—"the message that I tell you" (3:2). The prophet does exactly as told and arises and goes "in accordance with the word of the Lord," but his silence still conceals the content of his heart.

1. *to Jonah* Unlike the first scene, here his father's name is not mentioned, following the standard procedure for subsequent references to a character (see Comment to 1:1).

a second time In the story of Elijah's flight from prophecy and from life (1 Kings 19:3–8), too, the need to overcome the prophet's opposition is expressed by the word-for-word repetition of the divine instruction to him ("Arise and eat") and by the statement that it was given "a second time."

2. *and cry out to it* Whereas the first mandate used language that unquestionably denotes a rebuke—*qara 'al*, "cry out against" (see Comment to 1:2)—here the more general idiom *qara 'el*, "cry out to," fits the character of the repeated commandment, which contains no explicit statement of the reason for it, and is strengthened by the internal accusative in the Hebrew *qera'... 'et ha-qeri'ah*, more literally "proclaim... the proclamation."

tell you The *qal* present-tense *dover* is also used in the Lord's instruction to Moses—"speak to Pharaoh king of Egypt all that I *tell* you" (Exod. 6:29)—to emphasize the prophet's obligation to overcome his opposition and speak what he is about to hear from the Lord's mouth (cf. Deut. 5:1). By contrast, when the Lord speaks to Balaam, we have a *pi'el* (intensive) future tense—"But whatever I *will tell* you, that you shall do" (Num. 22:20)—to emphasize the duty to comply with whatever the Lord may say to him in the future (cf. Exod. 23:22).

In Doomed Nineveh: The Repentance of the Sinners   (vv. 3:3b–10)

The threat of total destruction that looms over Nineveh is like the peril of shipwreck that threatened the ship. But whereas Jonah remained aloof from the crew, did not participate in their efforts to save themselves, and refused to pray to his God, now he enters the city and proclaims to its inhabitants the message of their impending doom. Thanks to this explicit warning, which consigns Nineveh to the destiny of Sodom and thus indirectly indicts it for the same sins, the people of Nineveh do not have to go through the interim stage of uncertainty and inquiry that the sailors experienced. Their test is chiefly one of faith: will they give credence to the clear and explicit decree, understand what they must do, and be courageous enough to do it? In fact, not only do they give full credence to the cry out to it the message that I tell you." ³ Jonah arose and went to Nineveh in accordance with the word of

אֵלֶיהָ אֶת־הַקְּרִיאָה אֲשֶׁר אָנֹכִי דֹבֵר אֵלֶיךָ: ³ וַיָּקָם יוֹנָה וַיֵּלֶךְ אֶל־נִינְוֵה כִּדְבַר יְהוָה וְנִינְוֵה

word of the Lord as delivered by the foreign prophet (this is emphasized by the absence of any parallel to the sailors' questions about his identity [1:8]), they also recognize the magnitude of their guilt and endeavor to arouse the mercy of Heaven by afflicting themselves. For the sailors, casting the cargo overboard served primarily to lighten the burden of the storm-wracked ship, but it also expressed their recognition of the gravity of their situation and their preference for life over property. By contrast, the Ninevites' fasting and sackcloth serve no physical purpose. They constitute a spiritual and religious gesture that is meant to demonstrate their understanding of the utter seriousness of the divine decree and to repress the greed and lust that caused them to be so wicked. No prophet has ever had such spectacular success. Only a third of the residents of the city have heard his proclamation in person, but all of them, "great and small alike" (v. 5), submit to it totally and at once, despite the forty days of grace allotted them. In the wake of the popular response, the king (like the captain who completed the action of his crew) takes action and gives the force of a royal edict to his subjects' spontaneous actions, extends the obligation of fasting to the livestock, and adds the ethical dimension of ceasing their wicked behavior and making amends for past wrongs. The sinless captain sought to gain the attention and mercy of the deity who had sent the storm by means of his despairing prayer: "*Perhaps* the god will give us a thought and *we will not perish*" (1:6). Like him, the king of the sinful metropolis orders his subjects to call out mightily to the just God, in the scanty hope that the return of their ill-gotten gains might lead to repeal of the decree: "*Who knows,* God may turn and repent, and turn back from His wrath, so that *we do not perish*" (3:9).

The parallelism between the two scenes fails when it comes to the reasons for deliverance from peril: whereas the ship was saved from foundering because the sailors overcame their moral qualms and threw Jonah overboard, the destruction of Nineveh is averted when its people return from their evil ways and actually abandon the path of injustice. Whereas the men on the ship had to comply with the will of the Lord as a condition for escaping the "evil" (1:7) that had overtaken them through no fault of their own, the inhabitants of the sinful city of Nineveh must accept the justice of the Lord's decree and repent fully, in the hope that the Lord will relent from the "evil" (3:10) that He has decreed for them. Thus the symmetrical structure of the book unites two seemingly contradictory aspects of the character of God, the conjoining of which is the paradoxical theme of the book: the God who exploits His might to impose His will on His recalcitrant prophet and his traveling companions is the same merciful and compassionate God who forgives the vicious and wicked Nineveh for its crimes.

3. *Now Nineveh* The opening of a narrative unit with the circumstantial *vav* is not unusual (e.g., "Now Moses, tending the flock of his father-in-law Jethro" [Exod. 3:1]; "now King David was old, advanced in years" [1 Kings 1:1]). Even though here it comes in the middle of a verse, there is no doubt that the circumstantial clause is anticipatory, since it serves as an exposition that is essential for understanding the statement in the next verse about how far Jonah penetrates into the city.

was The past tense is relative to the time of the story and need not indicate that the city was no longer great in the narrator's own present. Since, however, the narrator could have written "Nineveh *is* a great city to God," with the sense of a narrative past (e.g., "Now Jericho is shut up tight because of the Israelites; no one is leaving or entering" [Josh. 6:1]), we may conclude that "was" indeed means that, in the narrator's present, Nineveh is no longer a thriving metropolis (see Introduction, p. xliii).

the LORD. Now Nineveh was a great city to God, a walk of three days. 4 Jonah began to go into the city, a

הָיְתָה עִיר־גְּדוֹלָה לֵאלֹהִים מַהֲלַךְ שְׁלֹשֶׁת יָמִים: 4 וַיָּחֶל יוֹנָה לָבוֹא בָעִיר מַהֲלַךְ יוֹם אֶחָד

a great city to God On a godly scale: "Everything that [an author] wishes to present as being very large is associated with God as a way of magnifying it; for example, 'God's mountains' (Ps. 36:7), 'cedars' (Ps. 80:11), 'Divine flame' (Cant. 8:6), 'Divine gloom'" (Jer. 2:31) (David Kimhi on this verse; see also his commentary on Gen. 10:9 and R. Samuel ben Meir on Gen. 27:7).

a walk of three days The ruins of Nineveh have been identified with certainty; the locals call one of the two tels at the site "Nebi Yunis" after the tomb of the prophet Jonah, which is sacred to both Muslims and Jews. The city walls, constructed by Sennacherib in the seventh century B.C.E. (see Comment to 1:2) and whose course remains clearly visible, are twelve kilometers long; the city's maximum width is five kilometers. It seems reasonable that a day's journey is thirty kilometers (even though the sages set it a third larger: "How far does an average man walk in a day? Ten parasangs" or about forty kilometers [B. Pesahim 94b]). Using this measurement, the diameter of Jonah's Nineveh would have been at least ninety kilometers. One can perhaps diminish the magnitude of the disparity slightly by accepting Abraham ibn Ezra's first gloss and understanding "a walk of three days" as referring to the periphery of the city and his "walk of one day" to its diameter (three being an approximation of *pi,* the ratio of the circumference to the diameter of a circle). Yet Ibn Ezra himself proposed a different reading that seems to fit the context better: Jonah "walked and delivered his message for only a walk of one day [i.e., only one-third the diameter of the city] and this is why [it is written]: 'Jonah began [to enter the city].'" Unless we say that the author purposely inserted this wild exaggeration, expressed also in the epithet "a great city to God," in keeping with the nonrealistic nature of the story (see Introduction, "Story or History?" p. xvii), we must conjecture that the reference is not to the duration required to cross the city in a straight line but to the period needed to traverse its streets and byways so that all the inhabitants can hear his proclamation.

4. ***Jonah began to go*** Here Jonah begins to fulfill the divine command. The infinitive "to go" emphasizes the antithesis to his flight, where we find the same verb: "to go with the others to Tarshish" (1:3; Tribble, pp. 178–179).

a walk of one day This indication of time also applies to the action in the next verse. Even though Jonah proclaimed his message in only one-third of the city, all "the people of Nineveh" responded. The rapidity of their reaction contrasts with the slow reaction of the prophet himself: he submitted to his God only after "three days and three nights" in the belly of the fish, but they did so after only one day out of three!

and he cried Even though there is no explicit statement that the Lord spoke to Jonah again and that the prophet is now delivering the message conveyed to him in that unreported revelation, readers have no problem filling in this gap in the plot. Alongside the frequent divine injunctions to prophesy that are not followed by an explicit reference to the execution of the command (e.g., 1 Kings 21:17–19), we find prophetic pronouncements whose revelatory source is not mentioned (e.g., Num. 16:28–30; 1 Kings 17:1 and 20:22). Moreover, here the narrator also echoes the language of the Lord's instruction to Jonah to "*cry* out to it the message [lit. '*cry out* the *cry*'] that I tell you" (3:2): "And he *cried.*" There is no divergence between what he was told and what he actually says; nor is there a subsequent divine rebuke of Jonah for saying too little. Hence it is likely that the extreme brevity of his proclamation, rather than being the sign of a grudging compliance, reflects the fact that he was not sent to reprove Nineveh for its sins, but only to inform it of the walk of one day, and he cried: "Forty days more, and Nineveh shall be overturned!" ⁵ The men of Nineveh

וַיִּקְרָא֙ וַיֹּאמַ֔ר ע֚וֹד אַרְבָּעִ֣ים י֔וֹם וְנִֽינְוֵ֖ה נֶהְפָּֽכֶת׃ ⁵ וַיַּאֲמִ֛ינוּ אַנְשֵׁ֥י נִֽינְוֵ֖ה בֵּֽאלֹהִ֑ים

sentence passed upon it. Verdicts of this sort generally include a statement of the crime before announcement of the expected punishment (e.g., 1 Kings 20:42 and 21:19–20; 2 Kings 1:3–4); but not every proclamation of impending doom is prefaced by explicit justification (e.g., 1 Kings 17:1; 2 Kings 20:1). It seems that here the indictment is encapsulated implicitly, but with perfect clarity, by the word "overturned" that forms the climax of the decree (see p. 29).

Forty days A typological number that indicates a relatively long period of time (cf. "I threw myself down before the LORD...forty days and forty nights, as before" [Deut. 9:18]; also 1 Kings 19:8). The suggestion that these forty days are specifically homologous to the forty days of the Flood (Gen. 7:17) is unacceptable, since that refers to the duration of the punishment, while here it is the period of grace until it comes due. This stay of execution presents an opportunity to escape the impending destruction. This may be by running away in search of refuge, in sincere belief that the punishment is sure to come, as Lot did to escape the destruction of the cities of the plain (Gen. 19:12–26) and as "those among Pharaoh's courtiers who feared the LORD's word" did in advance of the plague of hail (Exod. 9:18–21). Or it may involve a supernal effort to gain a pardon that nullifies the sentence, despite its certainty, as David attempted unsuccessfully during the seven days that preceded the death of his son by Bathsheba (2 Sam. 12:13–23) and as Hezekiah did successfully in the short reprieve granted him (2 Kings 20:1–11). That a sentence stated in absolute terms can be understood as conditional and a spur to repentance is proved by the Lord's admonition to Ezekiel: "When I say to the wicked, 'Wicked man, you shall die,' but you have not spoken to warn the wicked man against his way, he, that wicked man, shall die for his sins, but I will demand a reckoning for his blood from you" (Ezek. 33:8).

overturned Literally "is overturned": The present tense (like the prophetic past) gives the prophecy greater certainty and immediacy by invoking now the fulfillment that will come at the end of the forty days (cf. "At this season next year, you are embracing a son" [2 Kings 4:16]). Not only does the verb *h-f-k* connote utter and complete destruction (e.g., "he *overturns* mountains by the roots" [Job 28:9]; see also 2 Kings 21:13); it also particularly calls to mind the categorical punishment of Sodom and Gomorrah on account of their grave sins (cf. "just like the upheaval of Sodom and Gomorrah, Admah and Zeboiim, which the LORD *overturned* in His fierce anger" [Deut. 29:22]; also Gen. 19:21 and 29; Isa. 13:19; Jer. 49:18; Amos 4:11; Lam. 4:6). In the prophet's mind (and readers' ears), this comparison of Nineveh with Sodom reinforces the earlier one, "for their wickedness has come up before Me" (see Comment to 1:2). The suggestion that "overturned" has a double meaning (cf. B. Sanhedrin 89b), namely, that alongside the primary negative sense, to which the prophet overtly refers, there is also the subliminal possibility that the city will *turn* from evil to good—on which the inhabitants may pin their hopes (Tribble, pp. 180 and 190) or, alternatively, which readers can pick up (Sasson, pp. 234–237 and 346)—seems dubious. The narrator, in any case, does not call our attention to this latent ambiguity: the moral alteration of the Ninevites is expressed in v. 10 by the verb *sh-w-b,* not *h-f-k.*

5. The men of Nineveh believed God From the trust that the citizens of the wicked city put in Jonah, as the emissary of a Deity who punishes sinners in accordance with their deserts, we may infer that he did not merely repeat the short proclamation (five words in Hebrew) of the city's impending destruction, but made it plain that he was speaking on behalf of the mighty Judge of all the earth. The extremely elliptical believed God. They called a fast, and great and small alike put on sackcloth. ⁶When the word reached the king of Nineveh, he rose from his throne, took off his robe, put on sackcloth, and sat in ashes. ⁷And he had

וַיִּקְרְאוּ־צוֹם וַיִּלְבְּשׁוּ שַׂקִּים מִגְּדוֹלָם וְעַד־
קְטַנָּם: ⁶ וַיִּגַּע הַדָּבָר אֶל־מֶלֶךְ נִינְוֵה וַיָּקָם
מִכִּסְאוֹ וַיַּעֲבֵר אַדַּרְתּוֹ מֵעָלָיו וַיְכַס שַׂק וַיֵּשֶׁב
עַל־הָאֵפֶר: ⁷ וַיַּזְעֵק וַיֹּאמֶר בְּנִינְוֵה מִטַּעַם

description of how the prophet persuades the foreign city makes the vigorous response to his call all the more impressive but detracts from the realism of the scene (see Introduction, pp. xix–xxi). On the high seas, the advent of the storm preceded Jonah's explanation; consequently, the belief of the *"men"* in his God was manifested in "great fear" (1:10). In Nineveh, however, the proclamation that only forty days remained until its destruction came first; accordingly, the dread that "the *men* of Nineveh" felt of what lay in store for them was expressed as faith in God's power to carry out His threat—they "believed." (The psychological link between fear and belief is highlighted in "the people *feared* the LORD; they had *faith* in the LORD and His servant Moses" [Exod. 14:31].)

They called a fast   They proclaimed a compulsory fast (cf. "Proclaim a fast and seat Naboth at the front of the assembly" [1 Kings 21:9]; see also Esther 4:3, Neh. 9:1).

great and small alike   In the Sodom pericope, it is the all-inclusive scope of the guilt that is emphasized, "from young to old" (Gen. 19:4). Here the comprehensive guilt is overcome by the all-inclusive scope of the repentance.

put on sackcloth   The conjunction of afflicting oneself by fasting and by wearing sackcloth is commonplace in the Bible (see 1 Kings 21:27; Esther 4:3; Neh. 9:1).

6.   When the word reached the king of Nineveh   The rumor of Jonah's prophecy reached the king (a similar use of the verb *n-g-ʿ* in the *qal,* with the sense of "reach" normally associated with the *hifʿil,* is found in Judg. 20:34, Jer. 51:9, and elsewhere). To the king's credit, it is related that—even though Jonah never entered his presence—the monarch renounced his dignity and responded at once to the proclamation that had reached him only indirectly. Furthermore, not only did he surpass his subjects in his acts of repentance, he did not demand that they emulate his sitting on ashes. The antithesis of this royal compliance is found in the stubbornness of King Jehoiakim when he hears Jeremiah's prophecy of the destruction of Judah: "Yet the king and all his courtiers who heard all these words showed no fear and did not tear their garments" (Jer. 36:24; see the Introduction, pp. xxxix–xl).

the king of Nineveh   In contrast to the Assyrian custom and the dozens of references to the "king of Assyria" in the Bible, only here is he referred to by the name of his capital, as befits the urban perspective of the narrative: the king of Nineveh calls on its inhabitants to stop dealing unjustly with one another (see v. 8) and remains quite oblivious to the despoiling of the subject nations whose wealth enriched the capital of the Assyrian empire (see Isa. 10:14; Neh. 2:10).

he rose from his throne   The self-abasement of sitting on the ground (like Job's friends [2:13]) or even in ashes (like Job himself [2:8]) is an expression of mourning (like Job and his friends; see also Ezek. 26:16–17). It may also be intended to arouse heaven's mercies, as here and in the case of David, who lies on the ground for seven days during the illness of Bathsheba's son (2 Sam. 12:16–17; see also Dan. 9:3).

7.   he had the word cried   In the *hifʿil* (causative), *z-ʿ-q* generally means "call to an assembly, muster" (e.g., Judg. 4:10; 2 Sam. 20:5). Here, though, it means to "proclaim or spread a message" (Targum Jonathan renders it as "announced," as it does the same root and form in Zech. 6:8 ["then he *alerted* me"]). The narrator probably selected this the word cried through Nineveh: "By decree of the king and his nobles: Every man and beast—of flock or herd—shall not taste anything! They shall not graze,

הַמֶּלֶךְ וּגְדֹלָיו לֵאמֹר הָאָדָם וְהַבְּהֵמָה הַבָּקָר וְהַצֹּאן אַל־יִטְעֲמוּ מְאוּמָה אַל־יִרְעוּ וּמַיִם אַל־

verb to reinforce the formal linkage with what took place on the ship—in view of the danger of foundering the sailors *cried out* to their gods (1:5), while the king of Nineveh had the criers (cf. Dan. 3:4) *cry out* the message of repentance for his subjects to hear.

By decree Hebrew *mi-ta'am:* At the command of, as Targum Jonathan renders it, thanks to his familiarity with the Aramaic noun *ta'am,* which means "injunction" or "order" (as in "You, O king, gave an order" [Dan. 3:10]; see also Ezra 4:21). The medieval commentators (except for Joseph Kara, who glossed it as "the king's commands") did not realize that this is an Aramaism found only here in the Hebrew books of the Bible and tried to explain it on the basis of the usual meaning of *ta'am* in biblical Hebrew, for example, "by his counsel and knowledge and intelligence" (Ibn Ezra). Nevertheless, they were right that the prepositional *mem* here indicates the agent or cause, as in "it was not *by* the king's will that Abner son of Ner was killed" (2 Sam. 3:37). The words "by decree of the king and his nobles" are not added by the narrator but appear in the royal decree itself, which begins with the statement of its source of authority and validity.

and his nobles His ministers (cf. "all that were left of the House of Ahab in Jezreel—and all his *notables,* intimates, and priests" [2 Kings 10:11]; see also Nah. 3:10). Elsewhere in the Bible we find the inclusion of the king's counselors in the issuing of decrees only with regard to the kings of Persia: "you are commissioned by the king and his seven advisers" (Ezra 7:14; see also Esther 1:13 and Dan. 6:18). This is an important point for determining when the book was written (see Introduction, p. xliii).

Man and beast The inclusion of animals in the acts of mortification is quite extraordinary. The sages saw it as a grave misdeed—causing pain to animals in order to arouse divine mercy for their owners: "Rabbi Shimon ben Levi said: The repentance of the Ninevites was fraudulent. What did they do? Rabbi Honeh in the name of Rabbi Shimon ben Halafta: They put calves inside and their mothers outside; foals inside and their mothers outside; and these bellowed from here, and those from there. They said: 'If you do not have mercy on us, we will not have mercy on them'" (J. Ta'anit 2,1 [65b]). According to the *peshat,* however, their action seems reasonable and even appropriate and justified, since it is anchored in the Scriptural view that human beings and animals have interwoven lives and a shared destiny. The wickedness of human beings doomed the animals and birds to destruction by the Flood (Gen. 6:5–7); what is more, the deliverance of the human race from that decree involved that of the animals as well, and the end of that fatal cataclysm depended on divine mercy for both at the same time: "God remembered Noah and all the beasts and all the cattle that were with him in the ark" (Gen. 8:1). By the same token, we find that when the earth withers, both man and beast are affected (Hos. 4:3), that its conquest by the Babylonians means that "I even give him the wild beasts to serve him" (Jer. 27:6), and that deliverance is not complete if it does not comprehend the animals as well: "man and beast You deliver, O LORD" (Ps. 36:7). When Nineveh is overturned, man and beast will perish together. Accordingly the story expresses no reservations about compelling animals to participate in the fast (by not pasturing and watering them; cf. Judith 4:9–11) so that they will call on God in their hunger and thirst (for the notion that the bellowing of animals is a sort of prayer, compare: "The very beasts of the field cry out to You; for the watercourses are dried up" [Joel 1:20]; "who provides food for the raven when his young cry out to God and wander about without food?" [Job 38:41]).

and they shall not drink water! ⁸ Let them be covered
with sackcloth—man and beast—and call mightily to

יִשְׁתּֽוּ׃ ⁸ וְיִתְכַּסּוּ שַׂקִּים הָאָדָם וְהַבְּהֵמָה
וְיִקְרְאוּ אֶל־אֱלֹהִים בְּחָזְקָה וְיָשֻׁבוּ אִישׁ מִדַּרְכּוֹ

8. *Let them be covered with sackcloth* Unlike the three prohibitions in the first part of the decree ("shall not taste … shall not graze … shall not drink"), the second half consists of three positive injunctions ("be covered … call … turn back"). The repetition of "man and beast" is associated with the obligation to don sackcloth; since this seems somewhat ludicrous with regard to animals, some propose deleting the words as an accidental transfer from the previous verse. There is no textual evidence to back up this conjectural emendation, however. What is more, the repetition of "man and beast" has a literary logic, emphasizing that the king of Nineveh attaches great importance to the animals' participation in the effort to be saved. The validity of the king's premise is attested by the combination of "more than twelve myriad persons" and "many beasts" in the Lord's final reply to Jonah (4:11). As a matter of fact, there is nothing incongruous in the idea of draping pack and saddle animals with sackcloth (instead of ornate and comfortable saddle and reins; cf. "a horse … on whose head a royal diadem has been set" [Esther 6:8]). Only the cattle and flocks are really problematic. If they are included in the royal edict, one may conjecture that the idea is to make them look as if they are mortifying themselves and mourning, as we find in two Greek descriptions of extreme grief at the death of esteemed leaders. Herodotus (9,24) relates that the Persians cut the manes of their horses and beasts of burden. Plutarch (*Life of Alexander* 72) mentions the cutting of the manes and tails of the horses and mules in the Macedonian army. More striking is the parallel with the midrashic description of gentiles' ridiculing Israel and its God after the destruction of the Temple: "They bring the camel into their theaters, with its blankets on it, and say to one another: Why is it mourning? And they answer: Those Jews observe the sabbatical year, so they have no greens and ate this one's thistles, and he's mourning for them" (*Midrash Eikha,* Introduction 17). The king's edict continues by stating the obligation to cry out to God; it is not clear whether this, too, applies to the animals (Ibn Ezra rejects this possibility: "And they called out—the people did"). It is in any case clear that the duty of repentance refers exclusively to human beings, as is made clear by the word "person" *('ish),* which highlights the individual nature of remorse and atonement. A similar sudden transition from the plural to the singular, in a parallel context, is found in Jeremiah: "Let them turn back, every one, from his evil way" (Jer. 25:5).

call mightily to God Whereas the sailors called out to the LORD (1:14), whom Jonah had identified as the author of the tempest (1:9), the Ninevites are to call out to *Elohim,* an undefined "God," probably because Jonah never explicitly stated the name of the deity who sent him. In this moment of truth, at the brink of the abyss of utter destruction, the citizens of the great gentile city will proclaim their sins before the true God, even though they are ignorant of His name.

from his evil ways The king of Nineveh sees clearly that mortification of the flesh leading to submission of the heart is not sufficient. It must be completed by prayer and supplication and chiefly by abandoning the path of sin: "when My people … humble themselves, pray, and seek My favor and turn from their evil ways, I will hear in My heavenly abode and forgive their sins and heal their land" (2 Chron. 7:14; cf. Jer. 18:8; 25:4–5; 26:3–5; 36:3, 7; Ezek. 33:11).

and from the injustice That is, theft, fraud, oppression (cf. Nahum's description of Nineveh as a "city of crime [*or* blood], utterly treacherous, full of violence, where killing never stops" [Nah. 3:1]). The specific reference to social iniquity reflects the recognition that repairing the injustice is a precondition for forgiveness (cf. Isa. 50:1–2). The as-

God. Let every person turn back from his evil ways and from the injustice which is in his hand. ⁹Who knows, God may turn and repent, and turn back from His wrath, so that we do not perish." ¹⁰God saw what they did, how they had turned back from their evil ways. And God repented the evil which He had said to do to them, and did not do it.

הָרָעָה וּמִן־הֶחָמָס אֲשֶׁר בְּכַפֵּיהֶם: ⁹ מִי־יוֹדֵעַ יָשׁוּב וְנִחַם הָאֱלֹהִים וְשָׁב מֵחֲרוֹן אַפּוֹ וְלֹא נֹאבֵד: ¹⁰ וַיַּרְא הָאֱלֹהִים אֶת־מַעֲשֵׂיהֶם כִּי־שָׁבוּ מִדַּרְכָּם הָרָעָה וַיִּנָּחֶם הָאֱלֹהִים עַל־הָרָעָה אֲשֶׁר־דִּבֶּר לַעֲשׂוֹת־לָהֶם וְלֹא עָשָׂה:

sociation with Sodom is supplemented by the echo of the crimes of the generation of the Flood (Gen. 6:11–12), which we first encountered in the Lord's initial address to Jonah (see Comment to 1:2).

which is in his hand If the text read, "and return the injustice"—a transitive verb—the meaning would be that they must return any stolen property in their possession (relying on the metonymical use of palm and hand to denote control and responsibility; see Gen. 16:6 ["Your maid is in your hands"] and Exod. 21:16). Since here the verb "return/turn back" is intransitive, however, and followed by the preposition "from," the intention must be a more fundamental change—putting an end to the injustice that had become second nature to them (the palm as metonym for the entire person, as in "a stain sullied my hands" [Job 31:7]; see also 1 Chron. 12:18).

9. Who knows An expression of wishing and hoping (like the captain's "perhaps"; see Comment to 1:6), used by someone who knows clearly that even the most severe self-affliction (such as by David during the illness of Bathsheba's son [2 Sam. 12:22]) and even absolute and total repentance (like that demanded by the prophet Joel [2:12–14]) are no guarantee that the fatal decree will be revoked. This is because according to strict justice, even sinners who repent still deserve punishment, and the expunging of their transgressions remains an unmerited act of mercy. (Compare the self-abasement through which Ben-hadad's ministers hoped to attain clemency for their defeated king: "We have heard that the kings of the House of Israel are magnanimous kings. Let us put sackcloth on our loins and ropes on our heads, and surrender to the king of Israel; *perhaps* he will spare your life" [1 Kings 20:31].)

may turn and repent Change his mind and decision. The concept of measure for measure in the relationship between the purging of sins and God's repenting is expressed by the use of the root *sh-w-v* to indicate both what is demanded of the condemned—"Let every person *turn back* from his evil ways" (3:8)—and what it is hoped the judge will grant: "God may turn and repent, and *turn back* from His wrath." For another use of this rhetorical device, cf. "*Turn back* to me—says the LORD of Hosts—and I will *turn back* to you—said the LORD of Hosts" (Zech. 1:3).

so that we do not perish The king concludes his decree with a cautious hope that at the same time makes tangible the significance of the city's overthrow: we have all been condemned to perish.

10. God saw Like the king (see Comment to v. 8), the narrator too refers to the unnamed "God" *(ha-Elohim),* probably to emphasize that God responds even to those who do not have full knowledge of Him.

what they did In penitence, deeds have greater weight than words (cf. Isa. 1:15–16; Amos 5:14–15). Accordingly it is not written that God heard their prayer but that He saw their deeds. At first sight, the reference is to both physical mortification and the return of ill-gotten gains. Since however, the text does not say "*and* that they had turned back," it may be that "how they had turned back from their evil ways" is simply an explanation of "what they had done." This is how the sages read the verse when they cited the Ninevites' repentance as an exemplary model for what Jews should do at a public fast called because of prolonged drought: "What is the procedure on the days of fasting? . . . The eldest among them utters before them words of admonition: 'Brethren, it is not written of the men of Nineveh that 'God saw their sackcloth and fasting,' but that 'God saw what they did, how they had turned back from their evil ways'" (M. Ta'anit 2,1).

    from their evil ways Measure for measure: they "turned back from their *evil* ways" and correspondingly "God repented the *evil*" (cf. Jer. 18:8; 26:3); and again, "God saw what they *did*," and correspondingly God repented what "He had said to *do to* them, and did not *do* it."

    and did not do it The narrator's concluding words (*ve-lo' 'asah*) echo the end of the king's order "that we do not perish" (*ve-lo' no'ved*) (v. 9), to indicate that the royal decree and the Ninevites' compliance with it achieved their objective in full (Sasson).

CHAPTER 4

Outside The Pardoned City: Jonah's Second Rebellion (vv. 4:1–5)

Ideologically, Jonah rebels again because of his insistence that divine justice reign supreme and unchallenged. Psychologically, he is motivated by the death wish that assails him whenever the course of his life reaches the end of a blind alley: first, when the storm impeded his flight, and now, when the pardon granted to the wicked city undermines his confidence in the validity of the Lord's judgment. The gentiles in the story love life: their fear of death spurs both the sailors and the Ninevites to obey the Lord. But the prophet loves justice: his death wish prevents him from identifying with his fellow human beings and from making his peace with the ways of the compassionate and forgiving God. On the ship, Jonah opted for death rather than submit to the Lord's will (as the sailors did); now he again asks to die because of his displeasure with the Lord's mercy. As a result of their dread, the gentiles attain the religious humility reflected in the captain's "perhaps" (1:6) and the king's "Who knows" (3:9); but Jonah's yearning for death nurtures religious audacity. Jonah told the sailors, with utter certainty, that the sea would stop raging after they cast him into it: "for *I know* that this great storm came upon you on my account" (1:12). Now, indicting heaven, he asserts that he had known the final result of his mission from the start, because God's ways are transparent to him: "For *I knew* that You are a compassionate and gracious God" (4:2). The fundamental antithesis between him and them is further manifested by the phrasing of his challenge to the Lord's mercies, which inverts the king's hope that "God may turn and repent" (3:9) and recalls the sailors' prayer. When they said, "O *please, LORD*, do not let us perish on account of this man's life. . . . For You, O LORD, by Your will, have brought this about" (1:14), they were praying for deliverance even though they were about to commit what they considered to be a criminal action, because they were doing it in submission to the Lord's will. But when Jonah says, "*Now, LORD, please* take my life, for I would rather die than live" (4:3), he is praying for death because the Lord's attributes—so frequently stated to praise Him—are loathsome to the prophet, and his unwilling participation in their application has deprived his life of meaning. Alienated from God and man, he can only express his distress, voice his protest against the Lord's bounty to the wicked, and request that the death snatched away from him before the deliverance of Nineveh be granted him now that he has executed his mission.

    The Lord's rejection of Jonah's prayer is expressed in a harsh rhetorical question: "Are you that deeply angry" (that I pardoned Nineveh)? (4:4). The prophet's spiritual pain does not stir the Lord's compassion, either because it is of relatively small weight when measured against the threat of annihilation that loomed over the people of Nineveh or because of the grave error that has clouded Jonah's judgment. Not only is his wish again denied him; his defiance does not even receive the dignity of a reply. This divine rigidity reignites the spark of rebellion in the prophet's heart, leading him to juxtapose his own perspective—"until he should *see* what would happen in the city" (4:5)—against that of the Judge of the Earth—"God *saw* what they did, how they had turned back from their evil ways" (3:10). Once again Jonah is supremely confident that he knows what will ensue: the city that rushed to repent will backslide all too soon. He need only wait, which he does "east of the city" (4:5). The unnecessary geographic precision is probably intended to present his waiting in the east as an antithetical sequel to his westward flight. The rebel, who opted for exile in Tarshish, in the far west, now restates his protest by going in the opposite direction: instead of return west and going home, he camps out east of Nineveh in a desperate endeavor to prove that he is right and God is wrong. But why does he choose to sit in the shadow of a rickety booth outside the city, rather than dwell comfortably inside it? The most likely answer is that he wishes to remove himself from the scene so that the mere presence of the herald of doom cannot influence the course of events. When he "left" the ship he was seeking to prevent the destruction of the sailors on his account, even at the cost of his life. Now, he leaves the city so as not to contribute to the deliverance of its inhabitants, whom he judges as meriting death for their sins. Such is the logic of the man of abstract and detached morality, who has only divine justice before his eyes.

The Lord's attributes of mercy and compassion are expressed as a more or less standard trope that is always invoked to praise Him (Exod. 34:6; Num. 14:18; Joel 2:13; Pss. 86:15; 103:8; 145:8; Neh. 9:17). Only Jonah, the proponent of rigid justice, presents them as the reason for his flight from his God and disobedience to His command. The fanatical advocacy of justice reflects a strongly intellectual position that perceives human beings as having the capacity to know what is permitted and what is forbidden and endowed with the power to control their impulses, feelings, and desires. As rational creatures, they are graced with knowledge of good and evil and the ability to obey their intellects. Hence they are duty bound to accumulate wisdom and enhance their self-control. The stringencies of the law and its vigorous application, on the one hand, and a disdain for mercy and contempt for human weakness and limitations, on the other, are important spurs to the fulfillment of this duty. Divine compassion is perceived not only as unnecessary but as actually harmful, because mercy undermines the force of justice by detracting from the certainty of punishment and obscures the clarity of judgment by adding a factor that cannot be calculated in advance.

Jonah fled to Tarshish, instead of delivering the prophecy against Nineveh, because he was aware of the Lord's predisposition to mercy, so that the true purpose of the terrible verdict he was to proclaim to the inhabitants of the sinful city was to stimulate them to repent. The prophet, who wishes to reinforce the good and the just against evil and injustice, is unwilling to perform a mission that in the end will undermine strict justice. What remains of the rule of law when iniquity that merits annihilation can be wiped away by a few days of penance? Now, after he has unwillingly fulfilled his mission and his foreboding has been realized, thereby reconfirming for him the aptness of his judgment and broad scope of his understanding, Jonah once again finds himself at a dead end: on what can the advocate of justice base his life when the Lord Himself allows His mercy to overcome His judgment? He can only oppose his God by means of a bitter condemnation of His long-suffering nature and great mercy and a stubborn anticipation that the doctrine of mercy will soon be proved mistaken.

4 This was a great evil to Jonah, and he was angry.
² He prayed to the LORD, saying, "Please, O LORD!
Was not this my word when I was still in my own

ד וַיֵּרַע אֶל־יוֹנָה רָעָה גְדוֹלָה וַיִּחַר לוֹ:
² וַיִּתְפַּלֵּל אֶל־יְהֹוָה וַיֹּאמַר אָנָּה יְהוָה הֲלוֹא־

1. *This was a great evil to Jonah* Of all the scenes in the story, only this one, which presents Jonah's reaction to the pardon granted Nineveh, is syntactically linked to the previous one: it begins with an elliptical sentence whose implicit subject was stated explicitly at the end of the previous scene (Wolff). Precisely what Jonah perceives as a great evil is stated not here but previously—namely, the Ninevites' return from their wicked ways and God's repenting. The narrator does not write that it was "evil in the eyes of" (a common Hebrew idiom meaning "be displeased" or "think it wrong" [e.g., Gen. 48:17]), but that it was "evil to"; this unique construction, *va-yera' 'el,* occurs nowhere else in the Bible. The analogous *va-yera' le-* does appear; but in all books of the First Temple period it denotes causing damage (e.g., "Now Sheba son of Bichri will *cause us more trouble* than Absalom" [2 Sam. 20:6]; "They provoked wrath at the waters of Meribah and Moses *suffered* on their account" [Ps. 106:32]). Only in Nehemiah do we find *va-yera' le-* with the sense of "be displeased" (Neh. 2:10; 13:8). Because this seems to be the meaning here, we have additional evidence for dating the composition of the book to the Persian period (see Introduction, "Idioms," p. xlii). It is a very forced interpretation to say that it means "be wounded" or "suffer": in other words, that Nineveh's reprieve vexed him to the point that his great pain made him ill (Abravanel). An exact parallel to the intensification of the verbal clause "be evil" by the addition of the internal accusative "a great evil," as well as of the bitter irony of accounting good as evil, can be found in: "When Sanballat the Horonite and Tobiah the Ammonite servant heard, it displeased them greatly [lit., "it was evil to them a great evil"] that someone had come, intent on improving the condition of the Israelites" (Neh. 2:10).

a great evil The internal accusative reinforces the contrast between Jonah's negative reaction to the deliverance of the city and the sailors' positive reaction to the deliverance of the ship, it too expressed by an internal accusative (1:16).

and he was angry This is another link with the previous scene. Not only does Jonah consider the Lord's repenting from *evil* (the punishment) in reaction to the return from *evil* (the sin) to be "a great *evil*" (injustice), but the wrath from which the Lord turned back (3:9) is now the lot of the prophet, angry that the Ninevites were able to turn aside the wrath of the Lord.

2. *He prayed* For a second time Jonah yearns for death—passive suicide. When he told the sailors, "Lift me and cast me into the sea" (1:12), he was indirectly telling the One who sent him that he attached greater value to his rebellion than to his life. In the present juncture, when he entreats, "Now, LORD, take my life" (v. 3), he implies that even now, when he is at liberty to do as he will, he remains steadfast in his rebellion and longs for death. This is the second time that the prophet who refused to pray speaks to his God in supplication. When praying from the belly of the fish (2:2), it was an expression of submission to God's greater might; when spoken from outside the city of Nineveh, it is a protest against God's compassionate nature.

Please, O LORD The words of entreaty and direct address are separated from the body of the request (which begins with "now" [v. 3]) by the grounds for it (cf., "Please, this people is guilty of a great sin in making for themselves a god of gold. Now, if You will forgive their sin..." [Exod. 32:31–32]; see also Ps. 116:16).

Was not this my word The same expression is used by Reuben in Egypt (Gen. 42:22) and by the Israelites on the shores of the Red Sea (Exod. 14:12) to assert that land? That is why I hastened to flee to Tarshish. For I knew that You are a compassionate and gracious God, slow to anger, abounding in kindness, repenting of

זֶה דְבָרִי עַד־הֱיוֹתִי עַל־אַדְמָתִי עַל־כֵּן קִדַּמְתִּי לִבְרֹחַ תַּרְשִׁישָׁה כִּי יָדַעְתִּי כִּי אַתָּה אֵל־חַנּוּן וְרַחוּם אֶרֶךְ אַפַּיִם וְרַב־חֶסֶד וְנִחָם

the sequence of events retroactively confirms their previous position. Unlike them, however, Jonah does not quote an earlier statement that has now been verified, because silence was an essential part of his rebellion, from the beginning of his flight until the end of the three days in the belly of the fish. Instead, he alleges the correspondence between what has happened ("this") and his expectations ("my word" is equivalent to "my thoughts, what I said in my heart"; e.g., "Because I *said* I might lose my life on account of her" [Gen. 26:9]; also Gen. 31:31). In his opinion, this correspondence fully justifies his acting in accordance with his own word/thought and against "the word of the LORD" (1:1).

when I was still   For the Hebrew construction (*'ad* [=until] + an infinitive with a possessive suffix), compare "but Ehud had made good his escape *while they delayed*" (Judg. 3:26).

in my own land   Even if the reference is to his country (as in Gen. 28:15 and Josh. 23:13) rather than to his own estate (as in Exod. 8:17 and Dan. 11:39), the indication of time by specifying a place (with the emphasis that it is his own) indirectly expresses the enormous personal price he paid for his rebellion—leaving his land.

I hastened to flee   Auxiliary verbs that serve an adverbial function are usually in the *hif'il* (e.g., "You have asked *a difficult thing*" [2 Kings 2:10]; also 2 Kings 21:6). Sometimes, however, they are in the *pi'el* (here and "How did you succeed *so quickly,* my son?" [Gen. 27:20]).

For I knew   Unlike Moses, whose request was to know the ways of the Lord and draw closer to Him "pray let me know Your ways, that I may know You" [Exod. 33:13]), Jonah cites his knowledge of the Lord's attributes to explain his flight from His presence and ground his repeated insubordination (see Introduction, "Jonah and Moses: Flight and Protest versus Intervention and Advocacy," p. xxxix).

a compassionate and gracious God   In both passages that list the attributes of mercy (Exod. 34:6–7 and Num. 14:18), the attributes of justice are also enumerated ("yet He does not remit all punishment, but visits the iniquity of parents upon children and children's children, upon the third and fourth generations"), though greater weight is given to the former. Jonah, however, mentions only the attribute of mercy. We should not view this as a tendentious omission on the part of Jonah; the attributes of justice are left out of almost all biblical prayer that invokes the attributes of the Lord (Joel 2:13; Pss. 86:15; 103:8; 145:8; Neh. 9:17). The sole exception (Nah. 1:3) is part of a call for God to take vengeance on the Assyrian enemy. Thus when Jonah says, "For I knew," he is relying on the knowledge vouchsafed to Moses and subsequently consolidated over the generations, with special emphasis on the attributes of mercy. One of the links between the books of Jonah and Joel (discussed in the Introduction, "Echoes of the Prophet Joel in the Words of the King of Nineveh," p. xli) is that the version of these attributes cited by Jonah is almost word for word the same as in the prayer in Joel 2:13–14: "For He is gracious and compassionate, slow to anger, abounding in kindness, and renouncing punishment. Who knows but He may turn and repent, and leave a blessing behind." The verbal expression is in sharp contrast to the underlying intention: the Lord's compassion, which for Joel (and Moses and all who appeal to the compassionate God) is the basis of hope, is a source of despair for Jonah.

evil. ³ Now, LORD, please take my life, for I would rather die than live." ⁴ The LORD replied, "Are you

עַל־הָרָעָה: ³ וְעַתָּה יְהוָה קַח־נָא אֶת־נַפְשִׁי מִמֶּנִּי כִּי טוֹב מוֹתִי מֵחַיָּי: ס ⁴ וַיֹּאמֶר יְהוָה

slow to anger   For Nineveh, this attribute was manifested by the withholding of the punishment throughout the long years of their evildoing.

repenting of evil   This attribute, too, which appears only in Joel's version (see above) but goes back to Moses's supplication after the sin of the Golden Calf (Exod. 32:12) and the Lord's response (Exod. 32:14), was fulfilled literally in the pardon granted to Nineveh. In fact, the king relied on it in his decree: "Who knows, God may turn and repent" (3:9), and the narrator immediately confirmed that such indeed was the case: "God repented the evil" (3:10).

3. *Now, LORD*   The consequential "now" (cf. Gen. 48:5 and Num. 14:17) and the following vocative return readers to "Please, O LORD" at the beginning of the prayer, effectively bridging the long justification and introducing the body of the request.

take   Moses, too, asked the Lord to take his life when his prophetic mission turned sour ("kill me rather, I beg You, and let me see no more of my wretchedness!" [Num. 11:15]). Even more obvious and striking are the thematic and linguistic links between Jonah's prayer and Elijah's petition after he fled to the wilderness to escape Jezebel. Elijah sat down under a broom bush (see further on v. 5) and, before seeking refuge in sleep (cf. 1:5), "prayed that he might die" (exactly as in v. 8). Many of the words in his entreaty—"Enough!...Now, O LORD, take my life, for I am no better than my fathers" (1 Kings 19:4)—are echoed in Jonah's prayer. Many view these links between Jonah and Elijah as ironic, intended to mock Jonah's spurious reason (prophetic success) by contrasting it with Elijah's genuine rationale (prophetic failure). The perception of Jonah's suffering as absurd and even grotesque is a direct result of the second or third general conceptions of the story discussed in the Introduction "Universalism versus Pluralism" and "Prophecy: Realization versus Compliance," pp. x–xiv). According to our view of the story and its hero, however, the comparison between Jonah and Elijah is not meant as demeaning irony but as dignifying identification: Jonah seeks death, like his great predecessor; so far as he is concerned, his anguish occasioned by the Lord's leniency to the evildoers of Nineveh is no less than Elijah's suffering at the sight of Israel's backsliding. It is true that Elijah ascribed his failure mainly to his unsuitability for the prophetic vocation (which is why the Lord strengthened and encouraged him), whereas Jonah casts full responsibility for his success on the One who sent him (which is why the Lord enfeebles and unsettles him). But they do have something in common: both are zealous advocates of divine justice (see 1 Kings 19:10) and identify so strongly with their role that when they despair of performing it rightly, their lives lose all purpose and meaning. Elijah sought death because of his inability to influence Israel; Jonah, because of his inability to move the Lord. The midrashic sages added a poignant expression of the spiritual closeness between these two prophets, whose excessive zeal for the Lord led them to despair of human beings and themselves, by identifying Jonah with the lad whom Elijah resurrected: "Rabbi Eliezer taught: Jonah ben Amittai was the son of the widow of Zarephath" (*Yalkut Shimoni* 2,550; see also *Zohar*, Exodus, Vayakhel, ed. Vilna 1922, 197a).

4. *Are you that deeply angry?*   Although the primary meaning of the adverb *hetev* is "well," it often indicates degree and intensity (as in "I...ground it *thoroughly*" [Deut. 9:21]; see also Deut. 13:15); Targum Jonathan renders it here as "very much." When the question is repeated in verse 9 and Jonah responds, "so deeply that I want to die," it seems that the Lord does not doubt the authenticity of Jonah's suffering but rejects its justification: Is My bounty such an evil that it vexes you to the point of death? The

that deeply angry?" ⁵ Then Jonah left the city and sat
to the east of the city, and made a booth there and sat
under it in the shade, until he should see what would

הַהֵיטֵב חָרָה לָךְ: ⁵ וַיֵּצֵא יוֹנָה מִן־הָעִיר וַיֵּשֶׁב
מִקֶּדֶם לָעִיר וַיַּעַשׂ לוֹ שָׁם סֻכָּה וַיֵּשֶׁב תַּחְתֶּיהָ

rhetorical question expresses an implicit refusal to comply with the unfounded request for
death or discuss on its own merits the prophet's censure of divine mercy. The God who
moved the people of Nineveh to repent of their evil ways hints that His prophet should
repent of his excessive righteousness.

5. **Then Jonah left**   Since we are not told that the Lord informed Jonah that He
had pardoned Nineveh, many scholars assume that he, like the citizens themselves, learns
of it only after forty days have passed and the city is still intact. Since, however, it is
implausible that Jonah would linger in the city and risk being destroyed along with it, he
must have left it at the end of his mission and settled down outside its walls, waiting to see
whether its repentance had averted the evil decree. If that is the case, this verse must have
originally followed 3:4 (although it is hard to explain how and why it was shifted from
there). Alternatively, we can say that despite the *vayiqtal* form of the verbs "left," "sat,"
and "made," they are pluperfects that describe events anterior to Jonah's realization that
the city had been pardoned—"Then Jonah left the city and sat to the east of the city, and
made a booth there and sat under it in the shade, waiting to see what would happen in the
city" (cf. Ibn Ezra: "[The narrator] goes back and mentions what Jonah did before the
forty days had elapsed"; also the commentary of Tanḥum: "This verse should come before
'This was a great evil to Jonah.' Because, however, it is not good to separate the story of
what happened to them and his resulting vexation, the narrator first completed that thread
and only then went back to recount what happened to him after he delivered his message,
namely, that he left the city"). More plausible, though, is the assumption that the
remission of the punishment reported to readers in 3:10 was also conveyed to the prophet
by the Lord Himself in another revelation (David Kimḥi and Abravanel), which the
narrator left out because we can infer it from Jonah's sharp reaction to the Lord's change
of heart (4:1). This is only one of many gaps in the plot that we need not and cannot fill in:
the narrator does not say how long the Ninevites fasted or where Jonah intended to
procure food and drink during his long stay in his booth. These lacunae comply with the
normal conventions of biblical narrative about what needs to be stated explicitly and what
should be left vague so as to make the story more concentrated and focused. (There is a
similar lacuna in the story of the binding of Isaac, between the undefined destination and
its subsequent certain identification—"on one of the heights that I will point out to you"
followed by "Abraham looked up and saw the place from afar" [Gen. 22:2, 4]—which
forces us to the conclusion that in the interim the Lord had made the destination known in
an unreported revelation). If Jonah was indeed vouchsafed specific knowledge of the
pardon, we can read the text in the order presented and say that he leaves the city at the
end of his short conversation with the Lord and camps out in the booth, waiting to see
what the future will bring.

and sat to the east of the city   The seemingly superfluous designation of place
links Jonah's two appeals against divine mercy: just as at first he refused to perform his
mission and fled to the far west, now he refuses to consider it over and settles down east of
the city. And just as in the description of his flight Tarshish is mentioned three times in
one verse (see Comment to 1:3), here his renewed defiance is expressed by the threefold
repetition of the word "city." There is probably also a phonetic expression of this
continuity in the play on words *qidamti* ("I hastened"), referring to the past defiance, and
mi-qedem ("east of"), referring to the present one (see Comment to "east wind" *[ruaḥ
qadim]* in v. 8).

booth   Jonah made himself a booth (a stationary temporary structure) rather than pitch a tent (a mobile permanent structure) or build a house (a stationary permanent structure) to indicate that he remains east of the city only to follow its destiny and expects that his presence there will be of very short duration.

until he should see   "Perhaps they would not persevere in their repentance" (David Kimḥi). His sitting in the booth in order *to see* is the antithetical complement of his lying down to sleep in the hold of the ship so as not to see, for they are both manifestations of his stubborn rebellion. Sealing his eyes to the storm expressed his refusal to accept the force of the Lord's injunction; seeking new germs of wickedness in Nineveh expresses his refusal to recognize the justice of absolution. Jonah's hope that Nineveh will demonstrate that he is right and God wrong is the utter antithesis of Abraham's silent acceptance of the execution of the sentence when he goes out in the morning to see whether his appeal has been accepted: "looking down toward Sodom and Gomorrah and all the land of the Plain, he saw the smoke of the land rising like the smoke of a kiln" (Gen. 19:28). What is more, the contrast between the adversary of the Sodom-like Nineveh and the advocate of Sodom and Gomorrah seems to be intended. Of Abraham we read that "Abraham remained standing before the LORD" (Gen. 18:22) and even intensified this contact with God: "Abraham came forward and said" (Gen. 18:23). Of Jonah, on the other hand, we are told that he flees wordlessly "from the presence of the LORD" (1:3). This contrast is not meant to be critical of Jonah, however, but only to highlight the difference in the situations. Both Jonah and Abraham are courageous enough to appeal against the decisions of the Judge of all the earth—one championing greater leniency, the other holding out for greater stringency. Abraham's basic argument, that the Lord must not destroy the righteous with the wicked, was accepted; but the appeal itself was rejected on the grounds that there were not even ten righteous men in Sodom (see Gen. 19:4). Jonah was factually correct when he foresaw that Nineveh would repent and that the compassionate God would remit its punishment, and his expectation of what will eventually happen in the city is probably also correct. But the Lord utterly repudiates his basic premise that mercy must not be intermingled with justice. It is an error that cannot be eradicated from his heart by additional information, but only by personal experience that will open his eyes to a clearer perception of himself, other human beings, and his God. All of this will be accomplished for him by a plant.

East of Nineveh: Acquiescence   (vv. 4:6–11)

In the course of the night a plant grows up alongside Jonah's booth east of Nineveh. Jonah is overjoyed, because he understands that this miracle is intended not only to protect him from the sun but also to save him from his distress. Here "his distress" (*ra‘ato* [v. 6]) is lexically the same as the "great evil" (*ra‘ah gedolah* [v. 1]) he suffered on account of Nineveh's reprieve, and intensified by the cold rejection of his protest. Accordingly, he views its sudden overnight appearance as a sort of conciliatory gesture by the Lord toward His prophet. It provides a counterweight and remedy for his distress and anger, because he can understand it as encouragement of his struggle to demonstrate the justice of his path, or at least as an expression of the Lord's concern for his well-being. In the shade of the plant, the situation appears in a new light: despite the Lord's ironic response to the prophet's anger and despair, He is not indifferent to his spiritual distress; perhaps He, too, is waiting, as it were, to see how things will turn out in the metropolis. Proportionate to happen in the city. ⁶ The Lord God appointed a ricinus plant, which grew up above Jonah, to provide

בַּצֵּל עַד אֲשֶׁר יִרְאֶה מַה־יִּהְיֶה בָּעִיר: ⁶ וַיְמַן יְהֹוָה־אֱלֹהִים קִיקָיוֹן וַיַּעַל ׀ מֵעַל לְיוֹנָה לִהְיוֹת

Jonah's delight in the plant is his anger at its loss. The fish, which saved him from drowning, ultimately proved a means to coerce his submission. And now he finds that the plant, too, has been given him only to be snatched away at the first opportunity. His faintness exposes his physical fragility, emotional vulnerability, and total dependence on the arbitrary will of God. Once again he is stripped of everything except his longing for death; this time, however, he lacks even the ability to pray and beg the Lord to grant his wish. The wicked Ninevites with their lust for life had to learn through fasting and sackcloth how to make their bodily appetites and impulses bow before the imperatives of morality. The man of the spirit, who holds fast to justice and is zealous on behalf of law, must learn through sunstroke and unconsciousness that the living and vulnerable body is the bearer and maintainer of morality. The painful and humiliating experience opens his eyes to his reliance on his body and makes him aware that creatures of flesh and blood are ineluctably dependent on the mercies of heaven. Only from the depths of the physical and emotional crisis can Jonah respond to the Lord's explanatory and restorative speech. God's ironic question about Jonah's anger over the loss of the plant places his anger over the pardoning of Nineveh in its true dimensions. As a result, the fierce advocate of justice learns that he is biased in his own favor. His conscious and overt self-pity opens him to a comprehension of the Lord's compassion to others.

The Lord's last speech does not refer to the moral argument, and the question of the Ninevites' future conduct does not come up at all. At the end of chapter 3, we were told that the Lord forgave Nineveh because he saw that it had returned from its evil ways; at the end of chapter 4, He tells His prophet that, in addition, He felt pity for the city because of its immense size. Abravanel provides a pithy restatement of the tension between the two rationales cited for God's leniency: "It is known that it was because of their repenting that the Lord relented from the evil, not because of the children and animals" ("The Second Prophecy," Question 5). In fact, although the Ninevites' repentance was a necessary condition for their pardon, they would not have altered their wicked course had the Lord not sent them His prophet—for He does not desire the death of the wicked (Ezek. 18:23) and the destruction of children and animals with them. The crux of the Lord's response to Jonah is the comparison of the puniness of the plant and its existential nullity with the great magnitude of Nineveh and its existential moment. The plant was important to Jonah because it shaded his head and encouraged him; but what emotional engagement could he have to it when he did not toil to cultivate it and did not have enough time to become attached to it? If, despite its mean and ephemeral existence, Jonah mourned the death of the plant so strongly, perhaps he can now understand how Nineveh merited its Creator's mercy, if only by virtue of its size and the tens of thousands of human beings and animals living in it. Emotions cannot be explained; they can only be aroused. Only after Jonah rejoiced in the plant and grieved at its withering could his heart be opened to echo the Lord's rejoicing in His works (see Ps. 104:31) and His pain at their loss (see Ezek. 18:23). The *a fortiori* argument in the Lord's rhetorical question is more emotional than logical. Jonah's mute response indicates that he had no answer to it and may perhaps have ended his rebellion, recognizing at last the righteousness of his God.

6. *The Lord God*   There is no ready explanation why here and here alone do we find the compound name of the Deity. Some apply to this verse the midrash on the use of "the Lord God" in the Garden of Eden pericope, which does seem to suit the message of the Book of Jonah: "The Holy One, blessed be He, wanted to create the world by means of justice [i.e., by means of the name *Elohim*], but could not do so because of the acts of

shade over his head and save him from his distress.   צֵל עַל־רֹאשׁוֹ לְהַצִּיל לוֹ מֵרָעָתוֹ וַיִּשְׂמַח יוֹנָה
Jonah felt great joy about the ricinus plant. [7] But God   עַל־הַקִּיקָיוֹן שִׂמְחָה גְדוֹלָה: [7] וַיְמַן הָאֱלֹהִים

the righteous; He wanted to create it by means of mercy [i.e., by means of the Ineffable Name], but could not do so because of the wicked. What did He do? He combined the two, justice and mercy, and created the world, as it says: 'When the LORD God made earth and heaven' (Gen. 2:4)" (*Pesiqta Rabbati* 40, ed. Ish Shalom [Vienna, 1880], p. 167a). However, just as this allocation of these two divine attributes to two of His names is not supported by the Bible as a whole, it does not fit in with the use of the Divine Names in the Book of Jonah. The copresence of justice and mercy and the two facets of the strict yet loving hand are manifested not only in the incident of the plant but also in that of the fish, which also begins as a means of rescue and ends up as a bitter trap. Nevertheless, the combination of the two Divine Names is found only here, whereas previously we read that "the LORD appointed a great fish" (2:1). Similarly, the attempt to explain the alternation between the two names in the book as a whole by the assumption that *Elohim* refers to the undefined Godhead known to the gentiles, whereas the Tetragrammaton is used in contexts that refer to the link between the God of Israel and His nation or His prophet, corresponds more or less to the situation from the beginning of the book through 4:5. It is absolutely impossible, however, to make it fit this last scene, which begins with the combination "the LORD God" (v. 6), switches to *Elohim* (vv. 7–9), and unexpectedly concludes with the Tetragrammaton (v. 10).

appointed   See Comment to 2:1. It is clear to readers that the Lord's direct intervention causes the growth of the plant, its succumbing to the worm, and the blast of the east wind. Still, the narrator makes this explicit by the threefold repetition of the verb "appointed" (vv. 6, 7, and 8), just as in the case of the great wind ("the LORD cast" [1:4]) and the fish ("The LORD appointed" [2:1]; "the LORD commanded the fish" [2:11]). These explicit statements place all the Lord's actions that return Jonah to his mission, as well as its post-factum justification, on a single narrative plane; that is, just as the Lord sends His prophet to move the sinful city to repent, He also sends various of His creatures to bring the fugitive prophet back to Him.

ricinus plant   Targum Jonathan does not attempt to translate the Hebrew noun *qiqayon,* found only here, into Aramaic and takes it over literally. The Septuagint renders it as "pumpkin." The *Amora* Resh Lakish identified it with the bush from whose seeds castor oil is produced (B. Shabbat 21a). Daniel al-Kumissi and Abraham ibn Ezra offer both possibilities without opting for either. The advantage of the identification with the pumpkin, a vine with tendrils, is that imagining the plant as climbing on the booth resolves the difficulty of the duplication of the shade of the booth and the shade of the plant—a redundancy that has led many scholars to rather far-fetched conclusions (some invoke it to distinguish multiple sources in the book; others allege it as evidence to support shifting verse 5, which mentions the booth, to an earlier stage in the story [see Comment to v. 5]). It is very difficult, though, to interpret the words "which grew up above Jonah" as meaning "which grew up above the *booth*." Accordingly it seems preferable to accept Resh Lakish's identification and understand *qiqayon* as referring to a plant that grows wild all over the Land of Israel, known today as the ricinus or castor-oil plant (the oil produced from its seeds was called *kaka* or *kiki* in ancient Egyptian and *kikeôs* in Greek; the medicinal plant known as *kukkanitu* in Akkadian has not been identified). This has large palmate leaves and is characterized by its extremely rapid growth. The problem of the duplicated shade can be resolved by assuming that the narrator felt no need to clarify whether (a) the plant grew alongside the booth and supplemented its coverage or (b) the green roof of the appointed a worm at dawn on the next day, which attacked the plant so that it withered. ⁸ And when the sun rose, God appointed a quiet east wind; the sun beat down on Jonah's head, and he fainted. He

תּוֹלַעַת בַּעֲלוֹת הַשַּׁחַר לַמָּחֳרָת וַתַּךְ אֶת־
הַקִּיקָיוֹן וַיִּיבָשׁ: ⁸ וַיְהִי | כִּזְרֹחַ הַשֶּׁמֶשׁ וַיְמַן
אֱלֹהִים רוּחַ קָדִים חֲרִישִׁית וַתַּךְ הַשֶּׁמֶשׁ עַל־

booth had dried out and the broad-leafed plant replaced it (for other questions that the narrator left obscure, see Comment to 4:5).

and save him   The root *n-ẓ-l* in the *hif'il* always takes a direct object (e.g., Gen. 37:22); the indirect object used here may represent the later grammatical form (cf. 1 Chron. 18:6 [indirect object] with the parallel verse in 2 Sam. 8:6 [direct object]). It may have been preferred by the narrator, just as he omitted the conjunctive *vav* to reinforce the wordplay *ẓel . . . le-haẓẓil lo,* which joins the roster of wordplay in the other "appointment" verses: *dag gadol* (2:1), *tola'at ba'alot* (4:7), and *ruaḥ ḥarishit* (4:8).

from his distress   Hebrew *me-ra'ato.* The possessive pronoun indicates that the reference is not to suffering caused by the heat of the sun (which is not described), but to the particular "distress" described above in verse 1 as "a great evil" (*ra'ah gedolah).* Thanks to the miracle worked for him alone, this distress has now turned into "great joy" (emphasized again by an internal accusative in Hebrew).

7. a worm   He who commanded the plant to grow could also have commanded it to wither; nevertheless He sends a worm, because His way with miracles is to associate them with natural phenomena (cf. Elisha's question of the destitute widow: "What can I do for you? Tell me, what have you in the house?" [2 Kings 4:2]). Whereas previously it was a "great wind" and a "great fish" that were sent to return Jonah from his flight to Tarshish, now a tiny worm is sent to put him in his place (the other two divine emissaries in this scene, the plant and the east wind, are also of relatively small dimensions).

at dawn   In the brief interval between daybreak and sunrise, the worm managed to gnaw through the plant's stalk and give it a deathblow that causes it to dry up. The speed of its action parallels the speed with which the plant grew, as will be stated explicitly in verse 10.

8. east wind   The response to Jonah's protest vigil "east of the city" is an "east wind." Unlike the "great wind" that generated a "great storm" (1:4), the attribute "great" (which occurs no fewer than twelve times in the Book of Jonah) is not attached to this gust. The Lord does not "cast" this wind; He "appoints" it. Nor does it endanger Jonah's life like its predecessor but merely reduces his ability to withstand the sunstroke, causing him to faint.

quiet   The adjective *ḥarishi[t]* appears only here; its derivation is doubtful and its meaning unclear. The debate among translators and commentators derives from their prior assumptions as to whether the east wind mentioned here and the great wind mentioned in 1:4 are similar or not. Those who equate them include the author of the Qumranic Thanksgiving Scroll, who, clearly influenced by the Book of Jonah, wrote "like a ship in a *ḥarishit* rage" (*The Thanksgiving Scroll,* ed. Y. Licht [Jerusalem, 1957], fol. 7, line 5, p. 121), apparently meaning a ship caught in the tempest of a *ḥarishit* wind, and the *Amora* R. Judah (B. Gittin 31b), who derived the adjective from *ḥarishah,* "plowing," and understood it to signify that "when it blows it makes furrows in the sea." Those who believe that the two winds are contrasted include the Septuagint, which translates the adjective with the sense of "burning" (evidently because it comes from the east), and Targum Jonathan, which renders it "quiet" (deriving it from the verb *haḥaresh,* "be silent" [a stative *hif'il*]). The *Amora* Rabba (B. Gittin 31b) tried to have it both ways: he followed the Targum with wished to die, saying, "I would rather die than live." ⁹ Then God said to Jonah, "Are you so deeply angry about the plant?" "Yes," he replied, "so deeply that I want to die." ¹⁰ Then the LORD said: "You cared about the plant, which you did not work for and which you

רֹאשׁ יוֹנָה וַיִּתְעַלָּף וַיִּשְׁאַל אֶת־נַפְשׁוֹ לָמוּת וַיֹּאמֶר טוֹב מוֹתִי מֵחַיָּי: ⁹ וַיֹּאמֶר אֱלֹהִים אֶל־יוֹנָה הַהֵיטֵב חָרָה־לְךָ עַל־הַקִּיקָיוֹן וַיֹּאמֶר הֵיטֵב חָרָה־לִי עַד־מָוֶת: ¹⁰ וַיֹּאמֶר יְהוָה אַתָּה

regard to etymology, but to make it fit into the context of sunstroke he dealt with *haḥaresh* as a transitive verb (a causal *hif'il*): "when it blows it silences all other winds" (Rashi: "being very hot"). In the previous paragraph we offered contextual arguments in favor of a contrast between the two winds; accordingly we should understand the adjective as the Targum does and read "a quiet east wind," one that is quite different from the strong east wind that turned the Red Sea into dry land (Exod. 14:21). The dry desert wind's lack of drama is part of its message.

the sun beat down　　The worm destroyed the plant. With no "shade over his head" (v. 6), Jonah now is exposed to the combination of the east wind and the burning sun (cf. "hot wind and sun shall not strike them" [Isa. 49:10]; also Ps. 121:6).

He wished to die　　Literally "he willed himself to die." This idiom is found only here and in the story of Elijah's flight to the wilderness (see Comment to 4:3). There too it refers to the despair with life that precedes an explicit request for death. But while it is clear that Elijah's petition is addressed to the Lord ("'Enough!' he cried. 'Now, O Lord, take my life, for I am no better than my fathers'" [1 Kings 19:4]), and similarly in Jon. 4:3 ("Now, LORD, take my life"), here we have only a longing without a specific address: "saying, 'I would rather die than live.'" This is the climax of Jonah's rebellion: This time he does not remain mute, as he did on the ship; nor does he protest aloud, as after the pardoning of Nineveh. Instead, he repeats his craving for death without entreating the Lord, who has already turned down the request. This willful mutiny is the last protest he has the strength to make. The supplications of the sailors and the Ninevites were answered, but the gates of prayer are sealed to the prophet who asks only to die.

9. *to Jonah*　　In normal dialogue, there is no need to specify that the response is addressed to the previous speaker. Here, however, the narrator emphasizes that God is responding to a speech that was not addressed to him.

Are you so deeply angry about the plant?　　The Lord's question ironically echoes his earlier query concerning the prophet's anger over the deliverance of Nineveh. God extends his former question, "Are you that deeply angry?" (v. 4), with the words "about the plant," thereby belittling the source of Jonah's vexation. But Jonah is unaware of the irony. After refusing to dignify the former question with an answer, now he responds from the depths of his misfortune with the confirming "so deeply that I want to die" (v. 9), magnifying his anger to the limit. Thus Jonah unwittingly passes sentence on the disproportion of his reaction: the fact is that he was not nearly as troubled by the salvation of Nineveh as he is by the death of the plant. He confesses that the broad assault on divine justice did not provoke him nearly as much as the personal attack on his own well-being.

10. *You cared*　　The roots *ḥ-w-s* and *ḥ-m-l* (the former rendered here and in the next verse as "care") are synonyms that are often used in tandem to express a compassionate decision not to harm or punish (e.g., Deut. 13:9; see also Ezek. 7:4, 9). But both verbs also have the primary sense of averting destruction and waste because of appreciation and esteem (e.g., "*never mind* your belongings, for the best of all the land of Egypt shall be yours" [Gen. 45:20]; "the troops *spared* the choicest of the sheep and oxen for sacrificing to the LORD your God" [1 Sam. 15:15]; "don't *spare* arrows" [Jer. 50:14]). Jonah did not have mercy on the plant, but he was exceedingly vexed about its loss.

did not grow, which appeared overnight and perished overnight. ¹¹ And should I not care about Nineveh,

חַסְתָּ עַל־הַקִּיקָיֹון אֲשֶׁר לֹא־עָמַלְתָּ בֹּו וְלֹא גִדַּלְתֹּו שֶׁבִּן־לַיְלָה הָיָה וּבִן־לַיְלָה אָבָד: ¹¹ וַאֲנִי

Similarly, with regard to the Lord's attitude toward Nineveh, the accent is not on compassion and participation in its citizens' pain and suffering, but on commiseration with and estimation of life itself: He cares about Nineveh because he would grieve at its loss. Thus the Lord makes known, to His prophet and to us, that Jonah, in addition to his rage at his faintness and humiliation, cared about the plant itself and came to appreciate its value within the short span of a day (cf. Tribble, pp. 219–223).

which you did not work for   In which you invested no effort or labor in planting and cultivating (the verse ignores the benefit that the plant brought to Jonah because the analogy between the Lord and Jonah does not apply to this aspect).

overnight   Hebrew *bin-laylah:* The construct form *bin* (instead of the normal *ben*) is found in only two other places in the Bible (other than its regular use in *Yehoshua bin Nun,* "Joshua son of Nun"): Prov. 30:1 and Deut. 25:2. The compound *bin-laylah* occurs only here. Both Targum Jonathan and the Septuagint translated *bin* as an adverb with the sense "during the course of" (a usage found in Mishnaic but not in biblical Hebrew). But this meaning, which can apply to "appeared," does not work with "perished," since according to verse 7 the plant did not wither during the night but "at dawn" (evidently this difficulty led the Targum to add the idea of sequence: "That this night was and another [i.e., the next] night had perished"). Similarly, the attempt to explain *bin-laylah* as referring to the duration of the plant's life (just as *ben shanah* means "one year old" [e.g., Exod. 12:5]) suits only the first term (its appearance was short-lived) and not the second (its withering was short-lived), since in the actual circumstances we would expect "and perished a day old *(bin-yom)*." The same applies to Hanoch Yallon's suggestion (*Pirqei Lashon* [Jerusalem, 1971], pp. 156–157) that we understand the expression in the light of the Mishnaic Hebrew *ben-yomo,* "on the same day" (for which there is also evidence in Syriac): although it is plausible to say that the plant sprouted the same night, it is impossible to say that it perished the same night, since it withered twenty-four hours later. Even though the idiom remains obscure, the meaning is fairly certain: the entire existence of the plant was ephemeral and transitory, and just as it appeared without warning, it vanished without warning. Its swift decay casts a retrospective illumination on the wondrous speed with which it grew, since both are evidence of its humble nature ("easy come easy go").

and perished overnight   The use of "perish" (instead of "wither" [v. 7]) sharpens the contrast between the death of the plant and the deliverance of Nineveh, whose king had prayed "that we do not perish" (3:9).

11.   And should I not care   The antiparallelism between the two elements of the *a fortiori* argument is less than perfect, as the explanatory completions make clear:

You cared about the plant [the small vine],
which you did not work for and which you did not grow,
which appeared overnight and perished overnight.

And should I not care about Nineveh, that great city
[which I nurtured and grew,

which was built over many days and was not destroyed over many generations], in which there are more than twelve myriad persons who do not yet know their right hand from their left, and many beasts as well!

that great city, in which there are more than twelve myriad persons who do not yet know their right hand from their left, and many beasts as well!"

לֹא אָחוּס עַל־נִינְוֵה הָעִיר הַגְּדוֹלָה אֲשֶׁר יֶשׁ־בָּהּ הַרְבֵּה מִשְׁתֵּים־עֶשְׂרֵה רִבּוֹ אָדָם אֲשֶׁר לֹא־יָדַע בֵּין־יְמִינוֹ לִשְׂמֹאלוֹ וּבְהֵמָה רַבָּה:

The common format of the two verses—similar introductory statements followed by two subordinate clauses introduced by a relative pronoun—makes it possible to leave part of the comparison unstated. Readers must complete it for themselves and attribute to the great city everything that does not pertain to the small plant: it is dear to God because it is the work of His hands (as is stated explicitly about Judah and Jerusalem in the similar *a fortiori* argument in the words of the Lord to Baruch ben Neriah: "I am going to overthrow what I have built, and uproot what I have planted. . . . And do you expect great things for yourself?" [Jer. 45:4–5]); and the continued existence of the city has great weight because it goes back to ancient times and the dawn of history (see Gen. 10:11). Leaving this unsaid creates a "vacancy" in the second half of the *a fortiori* argument, which is filled by an elaboration of the contrast between Nineveh and the plant: unlike the solitary plant, Nineveh is home to many tens of thousands of living creatures—human beings who have not yet tasted sin, as well as many animals.

Nineveh, that great city   The Book of Jonah concludes with the word of the Lord, just as it began; but the same expression—"that great city"—serves in opposite senses: in the first speech it is invoked by divine judgment to explain the magnitude of the wicked city's iniquity, whereas in the peroration it provides divine mercy with a reason for extending the Lord's compassion to His many creatures.

more than twelve   Like ten in the decimal system, twelve is a round number in the sexagesimal (base-sixty) system. (This explains the otherwise difficult expression "*about thirty-six of them*" [Josh. 7:5]: it means "three dozen or so.") As a typological number, twelve indicates that a nation has its full complement in that it comprises twelve tribes (the twelve sons of Nahor [Gen. 22:20–24]; the twelve princes of Ishmael [Gen. 25:16]; the twelve sons of Jacob [Gen. 35:23, etc.]). It is also a factor of the number who left Egypt (5 x 120,000 = 600,000), which indicates a large population. Here, too, twelve myriad indicates a large urban population. A typological number loses its significance when it is modified by addition or subtraction (as attested by the anxiety of the eleven tribes after the war against the Benjaminites following the incident of the concubine in Gibeah: "O LORD God of Israel, why has this happened in Israel, that one tribe must now be missing from Israel?" [Judg. 21:3]). To avoid this, here the excess is phrased as the numerically vague "more than," meaning many more than 120,000. (The number of those who departed Egypt is augmented in a similar fashion without impairing its "roundness": "about six hundred thousand men on foot, aside from children. Moreover, a mixed multitude went up with them" [Exod. 12:37–38].)

myriad   Hebrew *ribbo*, a form found in Aramaic (Dan. 7:10) and Mishnaic Hebrew. It is used in the later books of the Bible (e.g., 1 Chron. 29:7; Ezra 2:64) to denote 10,000 instead of the *revavah* of the earlier books (with the sole exception of the dual form *ribbotayim* in Psalm 68 [v. 18], which is considered to be an ancient psalm); see Introduction, p. xlii.

their right hand from their left   That is, between good and evil. The manifest superiority of the right side over the left is reflected in two passages: "But Israel stretched out his right hand and laid it on Ephraim's head, though he was the younger, and his left hand on Manasseh's head—thus crossing his hands—although Manasseh was the firstborn" (Gen. 48:14); "a wise man's heart [i.e., mind] tends toward the right hand, a fool's toward the left" (Eccles. 10:2). Some scholars refer the inability to distinguish the good and beneficial from the bad and the harmful to the fact that as gentiles the Ninevites are assumed to lack a well-developed ethical and religious discernment or are not obligated to recognize the One God. In the Book of Jonah, however, the gentiles are described as rational people who are responsible for their actions and quick to repent. Hence it seems most unlikely that the last verse in the book would suddenly present a totally different notion. Normally, in biblical Hebrew, the collective noun *'adam* (rendered above as "persons") refers to an entire human population—especially when paired with the word "beast" (e.g., Josh. 11:14; Jer. 32:43). In the present case, however, context demands that the word refers only to a part of the whole population. Here we must evidently gloss it—following Rashi, Samuel ben Meir (on Num. 23:9), Ibn Ezra, David Kimḥi, and others—as referring specifically to children, that is, to those Ninevites who lack understanding on the ethico-religious plane (like the children who are not implicated in their parents' transgression in the incident of the spies: "your children who do not yet know good from bad, they shall enter it" [Deut. 1:39]) and perhaps also on the practical level (like the child Emmanuel before he learned to distinguish what was fit to eat: "By the time he learns to reject the bad and choose the good, people will be feeding on curds and honey. For before the lad knows to reject the bad and choose the good, the ground whose two kings you dread shall be abandoned" [Isa. 7:15–16]). If indeed the 120,000 includes only the children, the population of the city must be several times as large. Assuming that children consist of a fifth of the entire population, the number of the city's inhabitants must be 600,000, which is equal to the number of the Israelites who left Egypt. This huge figure evidently contributes to the nonrealistic dimensions of Nineveh (see Comment to 3:3). In actual fact, this number is twice the amount of the 300,000 persons who lived in historical Nineveh, according to estimates of the population during Sennacherib's reign (Sasson, p. 311–312). The favorable attitude to the lack of knowledge of Nineveh's children casts ironic light on Jonah's proud boast, "For I knew" (v. 2): the Lord cares for them because of their innocence that precedes knowledge of good and evil, but He torments His prophet to make him understand that *his* knowledge—factually correct but ethically invalid—is worse than ignorance.

   and many beasts   This is a resounding echo of the yoking of "man and beast" that appears twice in the royal decree (3:7–8). The citizens and their king extended the obligation of fasting and wearing sackcloth to their children ("great and small alike" [3:5]) and their livestock ("flock or herd" [3:7]) because both groups of innocents would perish in the total annihilation implied by the threat of Nineveh's utter destruction. At the end of chapter 3 we are told only that the Lord accepted the repentance of the sinners; here the Lord himself unequivocally states that He must care (also) for the masses of children and beasts who had not transgressed. The divine attribute of mercy, against which the prophet rebelled, has two facets: forgiving the transgressions of those who repent, and compassion for human beings and animals because they are living creatures (cf., "Your beneficence is like the high mountains; Your justice like the great deep; man and beast You deliver, O LORD" [Ps. 36:7]). The Lord's love for His creatures does not mar divine justice; on the contrary, it is an essential component of doing justice, because those who stand in the dock are flesh and blood. Throughout the story, Jonah's flight from his God has been inextricably linked with his flight from his own life. Now the Lord makes him aware of the dignity of life in order to restore the prophet to his full human essence. The Lord's rhetorical question needs no answer, of course (cf. Jacob's silence when his sons demand, "Should our sister be treated like a whore?" [Gen. 34:31]; also Job 2:10). Hence Jonah's silence by no whit diminishes his complete recognition that the Lord is right (cf. the story of Solomon and the baby, whose climax is the verdict and not its acceptance by the sham mother [1 Kings 3:27]). Like the Book of Job, the Book of Jonah concludes with the rebel's submission to God. Whereas Job's acknowledgment of God's righteousness is explicit ("therefore, I recant and relent, being but dust and ashes" [Job 42:6]), Jonah's is tacit. In utter contrast to Job, Jonah, although a prophet, is not a man of words; just as his flight was accompanied by furious silence, his return is manifested by humble silence. Expressing his compliance in words would again make him the judge of his Judge, so he adopts the mute language of which the Psalmist wrote: "To You silence is praise" (Ps. 65:2).

BIBLIOGRAPHY

Midrashim

Midrash Jonah, ed. A. Jellinek, *Bet ha-Midrash* I, Leipzig 1853, pp. 96–105; ed. Ch. M. Horovitz, *Agudat Aggadot,* Berlin 1880/81, pp. 14–35.
Pirkei de-Rabbi Eliezer, Warsaw 1852.

Jewish Commentaries (in chronological order)

Daniel al-Kumissi (the Karaite), *Commentary on the Minor Prophets,* ed. Y. D. Marqon, Jerusalem, 1957 (Hebrew) [Land of Israel, ninth century].

Yefet ben Ali (the Karaite), *Commentary on the Minor Prophets,* MS London, British Library, Or. 2400–2401 (Arabic) [Jerusalem, tenth century].

R. Judah ibn Bal'am, "The Commentary of . . . Ibn Bal'am on the Twelve Minor Prophets," ed. S. Poznanski, *JQR* 15 (1924/25), pp. 35–38 (Arabic) [Spain, eleventh century].

R. Shlomo Yitzḥaki (Rashi), *Parshandata: The Commentary of Rashi on the Prophets and the Hagiographs,* ed. I. Maarsen, Amsterdam, 1930; also printed in standard editions of the *Rabbinic Bible (Mikra'ot Gedolot)* (Hebrew) [Northern France, 1040–1105].

R. Joseph Kara, *Commentary on the Minor Prophets,* in *Rabbinic Bible,* Lublin 1897 (Hebrew) [Northern France, c. 1060–c. 1125].

R. Abraham bar Ḥiyya, *The Meditation of the Sad Soul,* ed. G. Wigoder, New York, 1969 [Spain, c. 1065–c. 1135].

R. Abraham ibn Ezra, *Two Commentaries on the Minor Prophets: An Annotated Critical Edition II,* ed. U. Simon (forthcoming). The standard commentary is included in all editions of the *Rabbinic Bible* (Hebrew) [Spain, Italy, France, and England, 1089–1164].

R. Eliezer Beaugency, *Commentary on Ezekiel and the Minor Prophets,* ed. S. Poznanski, Warsaw, 1913 (Hebrew) [Northern France, twelfth century].

R. David Kimḥi (Radak), *Commentary on the Minor Prophets,* in all editions of the *Rabbinic Bible* (Hebrew) [Southern France, c. 1160–c. 1235].

R. Tanḥum ha-Yerushalmi, *Commentary on the Minor Prophets,* ed. H. Shy, Jerusalem, 1991 (Arabic with Hebrew translation) [Egypt, c. 1235–1291].

R. Isaiah of Trani, *Commentary on Prophets and Hagiographia,* ed. A. J. Wertheimer, Jerusalem, 1965; also included in all editions of the *Rabbinic Bible* (Hebrew) [Italy, thirteenth–fourteenth century].

R. Joseph ibn Caspi, *Adnei Kesef,* vol. 2, ed. I. Last, London, 1912 (Hebrew) [Southern France, 1280–c. 1140].

Don Isaac Abravanel, *Commentary on the Later Prophets,* first edition, Pisaro 1520; also many later editions (Hebrew) [Portugal, Spain, and Italy, 1437–1508].

R. Obadia Sforno, *Kitvei R. Ovadia Seforno,* ed. Z. Gottlieb, Jerusalem, 1982 (Hebrew) [Italy, c. 1470–c. 1550].

R. Moses Alsheikh, *Mar'ot ha-Tzove'ot* II, Venice, 1607 (Hebrew) [Land of Israel, c. 1510–c. 1600].

R. Elijah, the Gaon of Vilna, *Sefer Yonah im Bi'ur ha-Gra,* Vilna, 1800; ed. Y. Rivlin, Bene Beraq, 1986 (Hebrew) [Lithuania, 1720–1729].

R. Meir Leibush Malbim, *Perush Gei Ḥizzayon,* in *Nevi'im u-ketuvim im perush mikra'ei kodesh,* Warsaw, 1875; also more recent editions (Hebrew) [Poland and Rumania, 1809–1879].

Modern Commentaries (in chronological order)

A. Kahana, *The Minor Prophets (Tanakh im Perush Mada'i),* Kiev, 1907 (Hebrew).

A. B. Ehrlich, *Randglossen zur Hebräischen Bibel* V, Berlin, 1912.

W. Rudolph, *Joel-Amos-Obadja-Jona* (KAT), Gütersloh, 1971.

A. Ben Menachem, in *The Minor Prophets (Da'at Mikra),* Jerusalem, 1973 (Hebrew).

L. C. Allen, *The Books of Joel, Obadiah, Jona, and Micah* (The New International Commentary on the OT), Grand Rapids, Michigan, 1976.

H. W. Wolff, *Dodekapropheton 3: Obadja und Jona,* Neunkirchen, 1977.

T. E. Fretheim, *The Message of Jonah: A Theological Commentary,* Minneapolis, 1977.

D. Stuart, *Hosea-Jonah* (Word Biblical Commentary), Waco, Texas, 1987.

J. M. Sasson, *Jonah* (The Anchor Bible), New York, 1990.

Scholarly Studies (in alphabetical order)

Theme of the Book

S. Abramski, "Jonah's Alienation and Return," *Beth Mikra* 24 (1979), pp. 370–395 (Hebrew).

R. E. Clements, "The Purpose of the Book of Jonah," *Vetus Testamentum Supplementum* 28 (1975), pp. 16–28.

L. Frenkel, "His Mercy Is upon All His Works," in *Perakim ba-Mikra: Derakhim Ḥadashot ba-Parshanut,* Jerusalem, 1981, pp. 223–237 (Hebrew).

S. D. Goitein, "The Book of Jonah," in *The Art of Biblical Narrative,* Jerusalem, 1956, pp. 94–103 (Hebrew).

Y. Kaufmann, *Toledot ha-Emunah ha-Yisraelit* II, 1, Tel Aviv, 1947, pp. 279–287 (Hebrew); abridged English edition, *The Religion of Israel,* trans. M. Greenberg, Chicago, 1960. pp. 282–286.

C. A. Keller, "Jonas—Le portrait d'un prophète," *Theologische Zeitschrift* 21 (1965), pp. 329–340.

L. Schmidt, *De Deo* (BZAW 143), Berlin, 1976.

Exegetical History

E. Bickerman, *Four Strange Books of the Bible,* New York, 1967, pp. 3–49.

O. Kolmós, "Jonah Legends," in *Etudes Orientales à la Mémoire de Paul Hirschler* (ed. O. Kolmós), Budapest, 1950, pp. 41–61.

Y. Libes, "Yona Ben Amitai as Messiah Ben Yosef," *Jerusalem Studies in Jewish Thought* 3 (1984), pp. 269–311 (Hebrew).

E. E. Urbach, "The Repentance of the People of Nineveh and the Jewish-Christian Dispute," *Tarbiz* 29 (1949), pp. 118–122 (Hebrew).

History and Realia

A. Ben-Yaʿaqov, *Holy Graves in Babylonia,* Jerusalem, 1973, pp. 99–108 (Hebrew).

M. Elat, "Tarshish in Isaiah 23 and in History," *Shraton—An Annual for Biblical and Ancient Near Eastern Studies* X (1986–1989), pp. 17–30 (Hebrew).

B. P. Robinson, "Jonah's kiqayon Plant," *ZAW* 97 (1985), pp. 390–403.

D. J. Wiseman, "Jonah's Nineveh," *Tyndale Bulletin* 30 (1979), pp. 29–51.

The Literary Genre

J. S. Ackerman, "Satire and Symbolism in the Song of Jonah," in B. Halpern and J. D. Levenson (eds.), *Tradition and Transformation: Turning Points in Biblical Faith,* Winona Lake, Indiana, 1981, pp. 213–246.

T. S. Alexander, "Jonah and Genere," *Tyndale Bulletin* 36 (1985), pp. 35–59.

D. Flusser, "The Esther Scroll and the Book of Jonah," *Maḥanayim* 42 (1960), pp. 38–41 (Hebrew).

E. M. Good, *Irony in the Old Testament,* Philadelphia, 1965, pp. 38–55.

G. M. Landes, "Jonah: A Mašal?" in J. G. Gammie (ed.), *Israelite Wisdom: Theological and Literary Essays in Honor of Samuel Terrien,* Missoula, Montana, 1978, pp. 137–158.

J. Licht, *Storytelling in the Bible,* Jerusalem, 1978, pp. 121–124.

A. Rofé, *The Prophetical Stories,* Jerusalem, 1988, pp. 158–164.

A. J. Wilson, "The Sign of the Prophet Jonah and its Modern Confirmations," *Princeton Theological Review* 25 (1927), pp. 630–642.

Narrative Art

G. H. Cohn, *Das Buch Jona im Lichte der biblischen Erzählkunst,* Assen, 1969.

N. Lohfink, "Jona ging zur Stadt hinaus (Jon 4,5)," *Biblische Zeitschrift* N.S. 5 (1961), pp. 185–203.

J. Magonet, *Form and Meaning—Studies in Literary Techniques in the Book of Jonah,* Sheffield, England, 1983.

R. Pesch, "Zur konzentrischen Struktur von Jona 1," *Biblica* 47 (1966), pp. 577–581.

U. Simon, "Structure and Meaning in the Book of Jonah," in A. Rofé and J. Zakovitch (eds.), *Isaac Seeligmann Volume* II, Jerusalem, 1983, pp. 291–318 (Hebrew).

M. Sternberg, *The Poetics of Biblical Narrative,* Bloomington, Indiana, 1985, pp. 318–320.

P. Tribble, *Rhetorical Criticism: Context, Method and the Book of Jonah,* Minneapolis, 1994.

The Unity of the Book and the Provenance of the Psalm

B. S. Childs, "The Canonical Shape of the Book of Jonah," in G. A. Tuttle (ed.), *Biblical and Near Eastern Studies: Essays in Honor of W. S. Lasor,* Grand Rapids, Michigan, 1978, pp. 122–128.

G. M. Landes, "The Kerygma of the Book of Jonah—The Contextual Interpretation of the Jonah Psalm," *Interpretation* 21 (1967), pp. 3–31.

The Language of the Book

K. Almbladh, *Studies in the Book of Jonah,* Stockholm, 1986.

A. Ben David, *Biblical Hebrew and Mishnaic Hebrew,* second edition, Tel Aviv, 1967 (Hebrew).

E. Brenner, "The Language of the Book of Jonah as a Criterion for Its Dating," *Beth Mikra* 24 (1979), pp. 396–405 (Hebrew).

A. Hurvitz, "The Date of the Prose-Tale of Job Linguistically Considered," *Harvard Theological Review* 67 (1974), pp. 17–34.

A. Hurvitz, "Diachronic Chiasm in Biblical Hebrew," in B. Uffenheimer (ed.), *The Bible and the History of Israel* (Y. Liver Memorial Volume), Tel Aviv, 1972, pp. 248–255 (Hebrew).

G. M. Landes, "Linguistic Criteria and the Date of the Book of Jonah," *Eretz Israel* 16 (1982), pp. 147–170.

A. Qimron, "The Language of the Book of Jonah as a Criterion for Its Dating," *Beth Mikra* 25 (1980), pp. 181–182 (Hebrew).

A. Rofé, *The Prophetical Stories,* Jerusalem, 1988, pp. 152–158.

The Text

P. Benoit, J. T. Milik, R. de Vaux, *Les Grottes de Murabbaʾât* (DJD II), Oxford, 1961, pp. 181–184, 190–192.

M. Breuer, "The Text and its Sources," in *The Minor Prophets (Daʿat Mikra),* vol. 1, Jerusalem, 1973, pp. XII–XVI.

E. Levine, *The Aramaic Version of Jonah,* Jerusalem, 1975.

J. B. de Rossi, *Variae Lectiones Veteris Testament Librorum,* Parma, 1798, vol. 3, p. 194; vol. 4, supplement, pp. 88–89.

A. Toeg, "The Septuagint Version of the Book of Jonah," M.A. thesis, The Hebrew University, Jerusalem, 1965 (Hebrew).